YORK NOTES

General Editors: Professor A.N. Jeffares (*University of Stirling*) & Professor Suheil Bushrui (*American University of Beirut*)

Toni Morrison

BELOVED

Notes by Laura Gray

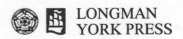

LONGMAN
YORK PRESS

YORK PRESS
Immeuble Esseily, Place Riad Solh, Beirut

ADDISON WESLEY LONGMAN
Edinburgh Gate, Harlow,
Essex CM20 2JE, United Kingdom
Associated companies, branches and representatives
throughout the world

First published 1996

ISBN 0–582–29347–2

Phototypeset by Gem Graphics, Trenance, Mawgan Porth, Cornwall
Printed in Singapore

Contents

Part 1

Introduction

Toni Morrison's life and work

Toni Morrison, a black American, was born Chloë Anthony Wofford, on 18 February 1931, the second of four children, in Lorain, Ohio. She grew up during the Depression. Both sets of her grandparents had moved north from the South. Her father, George Wofford, was originally from Georgia and knew the reality of racial violence. He worked as a welder in a shipyard, holding three jobs simultaneously for seventeen years, and was sufficiently proud of his workmanship for him to engrave his name in the side of the ship whenever he welded a perfect seam. Her mother, Ramah Willis Wofford, was a similarly strong-minded parent; when the family was on relief she wrote a long letter to Franklin Roosevelt complaining about the fact that they received insect-ridden grain. She took 'humiliating jobs' (as Toni Morrison would reveal in an interview with Nellie McKay) in order to finance her daughter's education. Toni Morrison recalls that her parents disagreed about 'whether it was possible for white people to improve'. Her father thought that it was not, while her mother was more optimistic, believing that whites might surprise them with their humanity. Despite this difference of opinion they both relied on their black friends and family, and, as Susan Blake relates in Morrison's own words, taught their children that 'all succour and aid came from themselves and their neighbourhood'.

Toni Morrison grew up in an environment steeped in black culture, ritual, music and language, in a family that encouraged her to believe in herself and be proud of her origins.

When she entered first grade at school, Chloe was the only black child in the class, and the only child who knew how to read. As an adolescent she read the great classics avidly – works by Jane Austen, Flaubert and the major Russian novelists – somewhat in awe of their grand style and their attention to detail. She graduated with honours from Lorain High School and went on to Howard University, where she studied English and Classics. It was here that she adopted the name Toni, because people found the pronunciation of Chloe difficult.

She joined the university drama group and took plays on tour in the South. Her travels there were a revelation to her, and a similar journey figures in her third novel, *Song of Solomon*.

In 1955 she received a master's degree in English from Cornell University. Her thesis was on the theme of suicide in the works of William Faulkner and Virginia Woolf. After this she taught at Texas Southern University for two years and returned to Howard in 1957 as an English teacher.

There she met and married her husband, Harold Morrison, a Jamaican architect, and began her writing career. She refuses to talk about her marriage which ended in 1964, when she returned to her parents' house with her two small sons.

She then became a senior editor for the publisher Random House, and commissioned autobiographies by Muhammad Ali and Angela Davis, as well as publishing fiction by Toni Cade Bambara, Henry Dumas and Gayl Jones. Her aims as an editor reflect her purpose as a writer: 'I look very hard for black fiction because I want to participate in developing a canon of black work ... black people talking to black people' (S. Blake). In the early 1970s she began to write for newspapers and literary journals, in particular the *New York Times*, where, between 1971 and 1972 she reviewed twenty-eight books about black life, and wrote articles about black life itself, including a piece entitled 'What the Black Woman thinks about Women's Lib'. She explained her career trajectory to Nellie McKay: 'All my work has to do with books. I teach books, write books, edit books, or talk about books. It is all one thing.'

If all her work can be traced to an interest in books, it is also unified by a passion for black history and issues of black identity. She has an academic and personal interest in race. She taught Afro-American literature and creative writing at SUNY/Purchase, Yale University. Her first critical publication, *Playing in the Dark* (1992), appearing simultaneously with her sixth novel, *Jazz*, is a probing inquiry into the significance of Afro-Americans in the American literary imagination. She examines the work of Willa Cather, Poe, Hawthorne and Melville and the dark presence within their writing.

Toni Morrison holds an unusual position within the ranks of black female writers, a group usually restricted to the fringe of the literary establishment. She has had amazing success in her life and work, and has received national and international acclaim. After *Song of Solomon* was published in 1977 it became a bestseller and won the prestigious National Book Critic's Circle Award for fiction in 1978. She has received an American Academy and Institute of Arts and Letters Award and featured in the PBS series of Writers in America. In 1980 she was appointed by President Carter to the National Council on the Arts, and in 1981 she was elected to the American Academy and Institute of Arts and Letters. In 1988 she won the Pulitzer Prize. In 1993 she was awarded the ultimate accolade, the Nobel Prize for Literature. Currently she is the Robert F. Gohoen Professor, Council of Humanities, at Princeton University. Her readership is wide-ranging: the appeal of her work crosses racial, cultural and class boundaries. Her novels are studied for their insights into both black culture and feminist theories, and are enthusiastically read by black and white readers alike.

Besides *Beloved*, which was published in 1987, she has written five other novels: *The Bluest Eye* (1970), *Sula* (1974), *Song of Solomon* (1977), *Tar Baby* (1981) and *Jazz* (1992). Their settings and themes gradually broaden. Her first novel focuses on young girls and the damaging effect of stereotypical white ideals of beauty, while her second novel deals with the theme of friendship between women. In *Song of Solomon* she extends her focus to include not only black women but a black man, Milkman Dead, in search of his identity. By the time of the writing of *Tar Baby* in 1981, a novel set in the Caribbean, New York and Florida, she is dealing with both men and women, black and white and their respective roles in contemporary society. *Beloved* has had spectacular acclaim for its intense and extraordinary features. It has been described as: 'a stunning book and lasting achievement [which] transforms the sorrows of history into the luminous truth of art.' (M. Rubin in *Christian Science Monitor*). It has also been hailed as: 'a milestone in the chronicling of the black experience in America' *(Publishers' Weekly)*.

Toni Morrison is now famous, and rightly so, for her mysterious blend of realism and fantasy, which is rooted in black folklore and her family's tradition of story-telling. She evokes place and culture with all the specificity of the writers she admired as a teenager, but place and culture of an utterly different kind – that of America's black underclass. In her writing as in her life, she is an anomaly, combining the highest professional success with a background of poverty and racism, appealing to both the general public and academics, and obtaining the success that many black female writers have been denied.

Literary background to her writing

The context for Toni Morrison and her work is clearly linked to her race and gender. She herself identifies a black style, an 'ineffable quality that is curiously black' (Nellie McKay) and her work is steeped in popular black culture, its music and folklore. Her novels juxtapose and combine joy and pain, laughter and tears and love and death. These same combinations are the essence of blues, jazz and spirituals, and were the themes exploited by story-tellers. The tradition of black female writers to which Morrison belongs is a similarly strong factor in her work. The first black published writers in America were female slaves: for example Phyllis Wheatley who wrote *Poems on Various Subjects, Religious and Moral* (1773) or Lucy Terry, author of *Bars Fight* (1746). The literary movement of the 1920s, known as the Harlem Renaissance, had several female protagonists, most notably Jessie Fausset who produced four novels between 1924 and 1933, while the character of Janie in Zora Neale Thurston's *Their Eyes were Watching God* (1937) heralds the advent of the black feminist heroine to American literature. In the 1970s the Women's Rights Movement and the Black Rights Movement intersected, and black women began to write about their experiences with a strong sense of autobiography and of female history, as can been seen in the works of Maya Angelou or Alice Walker. The existence of authoritarian and creative grandmother and mother figures – very true in Morrison's own case – have given rise to a conception of black female writing as a dialogue with the women of the past.

In terms of genre, Morrison's *Beloved* can be seen as having significantly different emphases from the slave narratives of the nineteenth century, a body of works almost 6,000 in number. These narratives contain a longing for freedom and self-respect while chronicling the slaves' life on the plantations, their suffering and eventual escape. Two examples of the genre are: *The Narrative of Frederick Douglass, An American Slave* (1847) and *Incidents in the Life of a Slave Girl* (1861). *Beloved* is not a personal account of slavery. Although the narrative consists largely of an account of Sethe and of her experiences, the reader is also told of the fate of all the inhabitants of Sweet Home and of various other protagonists during the course of the novel. Morrison's work is a composite story of slaves and of the general quest for freedom. However, she subverts the tradition of the slave narrative in various ways. Although the subject matter is the same, her purpose is very different. The slaves of the nineteenth century wrote with an explicit intent to effect the abolition of slavery. Naturally, those who had the power to vote for change were white, and the slave narrators therefore had to limit their stories for fear of offending the sensibilities of the readership who could be responsible for ending slavery. This led to inevitable compromises and caution in their literary style. The immediate pain of their memories, too, often resulted in curtailed accounts, rather like Sethe who skimps on details in her replies to Denver's questions about her past, and is successful in almost entirely blocking out the first thirteen years of her life.

Toni Morrison is writing in the twentieth century. There is no need to appeal for the abolition of slavery. Her purpose, however, is similarly corrective. The history of slavery must not be forgotten. Her purpose is to 'fill in the blanks that the traditional slave narrative left', as she explains in her essay 'The Site of Memory'. Morrison chronicles the psychological damage slavery inflicted on men in the figures of Paul D and Halle. However she concentrates on an elaboration of female pain, the history that is inscribed in the mental and physical scars that each woman in her narrative bears. The pain of not knowing one's children, of losing husbands and being continually at risk of sexual exploitation – the psycho-emotional effects of slavery – are elaborated in *Beloved*.

Black women can reclaim their history by writing about it, and the style of *Beloved*, which pays tribute to the non-literary background of black culture, places the novel at the very heart of this process. Toni Morrison uses different protagonists' varying visions of events to compile her history of slavery, and this can been seen as part of a contemporary trend to see history as multiple and inconclusive. There are significant gaps in her narrative: the past is not divided from the present, the two are interdependent and the boundaries between them are blurred. This is very different from the precision of history books, with their attention to prominent figures and the treatment of facts as fixed entities. It is possible to view *Beloved* as a 'history of the present', where the consequences of slavery's brutality are examined through the 'rememory' of Morrison's characters.

Historical background to her writing

Beloved, as we learn on its first page, begins in 1873, though the narrative stretches back to include memories of Sethe's mother, and Baby Suggs (Sethe's mother-in-law). Its protagonists are ex-slaves, though we witness their past as enfranchised individuals. Toni Morrison focuses on the issue of slavery by fictionalising the historical fact that slave mothers sometimes killed their children rather than allow them to become slaves. Such an event is recounted in the story of Margaret Garner, which appears in *The Black Book* (see Bibliography p. 72) a work conceived by Morrison and made up of newspaper cuttings, songs, photographs, recipes and other memorabilia, in order to produce a history of anonymous black men and women. Like Garner, Sethe kills her daughter, and attempts to destroy her other children in order to prevent them being recaptured as fugitives. She is successful in this attempt. Morrison says she wrote *Beloved* convinced that:

> this has got to be the least read of all the books I'd written because it is about something that the characters don't want to remember, I don't want to remember, black people don't want to remember, white people don't want to remember. I mean, it's national amnesia. (B. Angelo, 'The Pain of Being Black')

A regular slave trade between Africa and the English North American Colonies began in the early seventeenth century. Merchant shippers of New York and New England imported slaves as regular merchandise for the planters of Maryland, Virginia and the Carolinas. By 1670 both law and custom defined all Africans in the colonies as slaves. By 1776 the colonies had a slave population of more than 50,000, the majority based south of Maryland. The slave system began to come under criticism in the eighteenth century. In 1772, Lord Mansfield, the English Chief Justice, declared slavery illegal in England. Antislavery societies were founded in England in 1787 and in France in 1788 – but their efforts met with little support in America. After the invention of the cotton gin (a machine that separates the seeds and hulls from cotton fibre) in 1793, the subsequent boom in the production of cotton created a greater demand for slaves. While the transatlantic trade diminished, slave owners took to breeding their own slaves. Some states, for example Virginia in 1832, were so successful in this enterprise that they were able to export as many as 6,000 slaves. Organised merchant firms and slave markets were established. Despite the legal cessation of the slave trade after 1808, slaves continued to be imported from Africa. By 1860, the American slave population numbered well over 3 million. During the nineteenth century, the institution came under attack from religious groups and from secular politicians with humanitarian motives.

In America, the problem of slavery was a provocative political issue between the pro-abolitionist North and the pro-slavery South, especially over the question of refugee slaves. The Supreme Court Decision of 1857 appeared to give slavery new legal support and set the stage for the Civil War that raged between Northern and Southern states in America from 1861 to 1865. The Union forces of the North won the war in 1865 and the Thirteenth Amendment in the Constitution (1865) abolished slavery in the United States. Slavery, however, was not the main motivation for the Civil War. Northern and southern states, because of their geographical positions, had very different economic interests. The South was largely dependent on agricultural produce while the North was more urban and industrialised. Northern manufacturers wanted customs duties to be placed on foreign goods that they were able to produce themselves, while the South desired the free importation of goods. As the population of the North grew, the South feared that it would always be outvoted in Congress. In 1860, shortly after Lincoln became president, South Carolina and several other slave-holding states which came to be known as the Confederate States, claimed their independence and seceded from the Union. After a Confederate attack on a federal arsenal at Fort Sumtner, April 1861, the Civil War began. Originally the North fought in order to restore the Union, while their secondary aim was the freeing of all slaves, a motive which gained momentum as the war progressed. Finally, in 1865, General Robert E. Lee, on behalf of the Southern Confederacy, surrendered to Ulysses Grant, the Northern general. Even after the end of the Civil War and the abolition of slavery, persecution and injustice were still very much part of black people's lives. In *Beloved* it is 1874 when Stamp Paid reflects on the continuation of oppression long after slavery itself has ended.

> Whole towns wiped clean of Negroes: eighty-seven lynchings in one year alone in Kentucky; four colored schools burnt to the ground: grown

men whipped like children, children whipped like adults, black women raped ... (p. 180)

Paul D fought on both sides in the Civil War, and was never paid for his services. At the close of the war, he remembers seeing twelve dead black people on an eighteen-mile stretch of road (p. 269).

After the Thirteenth Amendment the North imposed Reconstruction – a period of racial readjustment – on the South that lasted from 1865 to 1877. Four million emancipated blacks were granted the social and legal rights that Southern whites had felt to be their own. As a response the KKK (Ku Klux Klan) was formed in 1866. The end of Reconstruction inaugurated a political climate of fear for black people in the States. Between 1882 and 1903 over 2,000 black people were lynched. The attitudes that had allowed slavery to exist resurfaced in the opposition to the Civil Rights Movements of the 1950s and persist to this day in extremist right-wing groups and racist attacks.

James Baldwin (1924–87) a famous black writer and social activist, writes in *Notes of a Native Son* (1955) that 'The past is all that makes the present coherent'. History plays a crucial role in shaping identity, both black and white. The history of slavery is personally significant for Morrison and for all black and white people. The past must not be neglected or forgotten, and Morrison sets herself against the 'national amnesia' she perceives as surrounding the issue of slavery. For Morrison, black history is the core of black identity. As Susan Blake has pointed out, it is not a case of 'forging new myths' but of 're-discovering the old ones'. In this process lies the clue not only to 'the way we really were' but to 'the way we really are'.

A note on the text

Beloved was first published in 1987 by Knopf, New York. The edition used in preparing this guide, and to which the page references refer, is the UK Picador edition published in 1988 by Pan Books, London, in association with Chatto and Windus, London.

Part 2

Summaries
of BELOVED

A general summary

The plot of *Beloved* is very difficult to summarise. Toni Morrison's technique is to thread various narratives together, using the present tense to convey the vividness of the memories of her characters. In the broadest sense, the novel recounts the story of a visitation from the past and the consequent upheaval in the emotional lives of the characters of the book. It is set during an appalling period in America's history: the years of the Civil War and of slavery. After the Civil War ended, in the latter half of the nineteenth century, life was still dreadful for black people, whether slaves or freed. Toni Morrison chooses to examine the impact of slavery on her characters since she believes that it is a subject that must not be forgotten.

Sethe is the main protagonist of the novel. She is a slave on a farm in Kentucky called Sweet Home. The other slaves who belong to the farm are three half-brothers called Paul A, Paul D, and Paul F, and two other men, Sixo and Halle. The latter becomes Sethe's husband. While their owner Mr Garner is alive, the slaves enjoy a relatively stable way of life. Garner prides himself on treating his slaves as men. He allows them to use guns and to hunt to supplement their rations and he lets them choose their own partners, rather than breeding from them for offspring. Unfortunately he dies unexpectedly and Sweet Home is taken over by his brother-in-law, Schoolteacher. Schoolteacher regards his slaves as animals and, aided by his nephews, submits them to various investigations and experiments. He will not allow them to use guns and ties up Sixo for having killed a young pig.

As the quality of their lives deteriorates, the slaves decide to escape. Paul D and Sethe are the only two who succeed. The other Pauls are killed, and Sixo is shot when the white men are unable to burn him alive. Halle witnesses Sethe's rape and beating by the nephews, and is reduced to a wreck. We assume that he also dies. Paul D is sold and spends several months in a prison camp in Georgia because he attempted to kill his new master. He manages to escape with the other members of the chain gang. Sethe, heavily pregnant with her fourth child, sends her other three children ahead to her mother-in-law's house. Sethe runs away on foot after being beaten viciously and being sexually exploited by Schoolteacher's nephews. She survives the journey and is helped by a white girl. She gives birth to her second daughter, Denver, on the banks of the Ohio. Helped by Ella and Stamp Paid, two black people who assist runaways, she arrives at Halle's mother's house in Cincinnati and is re-united with her other children. Halle's mother is known as Baby Suggs: she used to live at Sweet Home until Halle bought her freedom. In Cincinnati she has become an unofficial preacher and a significant figure in the local black community.

After only twenty-eight days of stolen liberty, Schoolteacher comes to retrieve Sethe. Rather than allow her four children to submit to the sexual abuse, exploitation and indignity that she has had to suffer, she takes them to the woodshed and tries to kill them. She intends to commit suicide herself. She is successful in despatching only one of her children to 'safety' – the eldest girl, whose throat she cuts with a handsaw. The two boys, Howard and Buglar, survive. They are absent during the narrative of the novel since they both ran away when they were thirteen years old. Sethe is prevented just in time from smashing Denver's head against the wall. She goes to prison with Denver and is saved from being hanged by the exertions of the Bodwins and various societies in favour of the abolition of slavery. These facts only appear as the narrative unfolds.

Beloved begins almost twenty years after these events are supposed to have happened. Sethe is still living in the house on 124 Bluestone Road with her remaining daughter, Denver. The two women are ostracised by the other members of the black community. Baby Suggs has died, after having given up her social and familial responsibilities. The house is rocked by the spite of the baby girl's ghost, who engages in poltergeist activities; it is saturated with an atmosphere of misery, manifested by pools of red light. In the first section Sethe wishes that her daughter would come back and allow her to explain her dramatic action. The novel charts this very event. A girl arrives whom Sethe and Denver gradually come to accept as the ghost made flesh. She calls herself Beloved: this is the name engraved on the baby's gravestone. The other inhabitant of 124 Bluestone Road is Paul D, who arrives to visit Sethe. He and Sethe have a relationship and he is as antagonistic towards the living Beloved, as he was to the ghost, whom he banished from the house on the day of his arrival. Denver, who has been lonely for many years, is dependent on Beloved, and resentful of Paul D. Stamp Paid decides to tell Paul D of Sethe's crime and the period that she spent in prison. Paul D is awed and repelled by Sethe's reaction to the realities of black existence, and leaves the house.

After his departure, Sethe is positive that Beloved is her daughter and slowly relinquishes everyday life. She loses her job in a restaurant and spends each day trying to compensate and justify herself to Beloved. The three women lock themselves into the house in a deadlock of love, blame and guilt. Beloved grows fatter and fatter while Sethe shrinks away to nothing. Denver realises that she must do something, and braves the outside world to look for a job. She is waiting to be collected by her new employer, when the women of the area come to Sethe's rescue. They have heard of the presence of the ghost and are determined to rid the house of Beloved. As they are gathered outside the house, Mr Bodwin appears. He is a white man who has helped three consecutive generations of Baby Suggs's family, and arrives to pick up Denver. Sethe lunges at him with an ice-pick, convinced that he is another danger to her children, and is only prevented from hitting him by being struck by one of the other women. Beloved disappears.

Later Paul D comes to visit Sethe and finds her lying in Baby Suggs's bed. He washes her and tells her that their shared past must be overcome. She must stop grieving for the death of her child, and begin to value herself. The novel ends with the possibility of a future life for Sethe, Denver and Paul D. There is an epilogue which commemorates the way in which the novel's protagonists forget their supernatural visitation.

Detailed summaries

Preliminary pages

These pages contain quotations which have great bearing on the text.

NOTES AND GLOSSARY:

Sixty Million and more: a reference to those who died on the long voyage from Africa to America during the period of slavery. Morrison dedicates her novel to the dead

I will call them . . .: this passage from the Bible draws out the irony of the name of one of the protagonists of the novel. Beloved is called into being by her mother, Sethe, and the novel is named after her

---

ONE   Section 1   p. 3

Many of the events which are later unravelled in the novel are presented. The time-scale is elastic. References are elliptic: coherence is denied and details are given that will only be contextualised during the course of the novel. We are introduced to a time and a place. The year in which the narrative is located is 'by 1873', and the place is 124 Bluestone Road, in Ohio, although before 1873 it did not have that number. The house is inhabited by Sethe and her two daughters: one is the eighteen-year-old Denver, while the other is the spirit of a toddler known as Beloved. Sethe wishes that Beloved could appear, so that she would have the opportunity to explain everything to her. Previously Sethe's mother-in-law, Baby Suggs, also lived there. Her death and a few fragments of her life are recounted. She had had eight children: 'four taken, four chased'. Sethe tells us in her present-tense narrative that Baby Suggs took to her bed and to 'pondering color', some nine years ago. We witness a conversation between Sethe and 'girl Denver', aged ten, as they try to summon up the baby ghost shortly after Baby Suggs has died. Sethe's two sons, Howard and Buglar, also lived in 124, but they ran away before they reached thirteen years of age because of the spite of the ghost. The house is avoided; neighbours gallop past and there are very few visitors and even fewer friends. We hear about the pink-flecked stone of Beloved's grave and learn that her throat was cut. Sethe pays for the wording on the headstone by having sex with the stone-mason.

Sethe arrives at her house to find a man sitting on the porch. Paul D has not seen Sethe for nineteen years. He and Sethe used to live and work as slaves on an estate called Sweet Home. As Sethe makes bread she explains that she has a 'tree' on her back, composed of scars that remained after a brutal beating. We learn that she escaped from Sweet Home while she was pregnant with Denver. She was 'nursed' by two white boys who stole the milk from her swollen breasts. Her other three children: Beloved, Howard and Buglar, were already on their way to stay with Baby Suggs in 124. A 'whitegirl' helped her. We learn that her husband and the father of her children is called Halle. He and Paul D were two of five men who 'belonged' to Sweet Home and its proprietors, the Garners. As black people they were possessions: Sethe herself was a 'timely present' compensating for the loss of Baby Suggs, whom Halle bought out of slavery.

As Paul D walks into the house he is conscious of 'evil', and feels the sadness that possesses the house. Denver is excluded from the shared memories of her mother and Paul D. She feels as lonely and rebuked as she claims the ghost is, denied the company of her brothers and of other children. She tells Sethe that she cannot live in the house any more. She cries, and later so does her mother. Paul D holds Sethe and kisses her scarred back. As a consequence, the house is rocked by the ghost. Paul D reacts to its presence and throws the furniture about, shouting at the spirit. Denver is half-exalted by the emanation, but is left eating burnt bread and jam from a broken jar as her mother and the stranger go upstairs to make love.

NOTES AND GLOSSARY:

124: the number of the house in the street

as soon as merely ... shattered it and **as soon as two tiny ... cake:** these are unfriendly manifestations made by the spirit that possesses the house

pondering color: it will become clear later that Baby Suggs is now noticing the colour of things for the first time in her life

Ohio: a north central state of America

the outrageous behaviour of that place: the behaviour of the unfriendly spirit

slop jars: containers for dirty water etc. – the house would not have had an indoor drain

rutting: an animal expression for mating

abolitionist: an advocate for the abolition of slavery

palsied: convulsed, shaking. Palsy is a human sickness – the house has taken on human qualities

chamomile: a wild aromatic herb

washboard: a corrugated wooden board for rubbing washing against

Boys hanging . . . sycamores: reference to lynchings

soughing: swaying and murmuring in the wind

Can't baby feet: can't pamper feet

looking for velvet: obscure here but explained in Section 3 where the white girl Amy who rescues Sethe is on her way to Boston to buy velvet

had sold his brother: sold him as a slave

Negro: in the nineteenth century this was considered a polite word for black; now derogatory

stroppin: strapping

niggers: derogatory word for black

Halle bought . . . years of Sundays: Halle worked on Sundays for years to buy his mother's, Baby Suggs's, freedom

speaker: a kind of lay preacher

hazelnut man: man with light brown skin

kindlin: kindling wood for lighting a fire

a look of snow: an icy look

haint: a spirit, a spook

the keeping room: parlour or sitting room

smoking papers: cigarette papers

chokecherry tree: a sour cherry tree native to America

They used cowhide on you: they used a cowhide whip

jelly: (*American*) jam

die-witch! stories: children's stories and incantations to banish evil spirits

---

ONE   **Section 2   p. 20**

Sethe and Paul D have sex, hardly having time to take their clothes off, and lie next to each other, embarrassed and shy at their abandonment. Paul D is repelled by the flabby breasts which he had supported so reverently before, and is disgusted by the scars on Sethe's back. As they lie next to

each other Paul D remembers one of the other Sweet Home men who was
called Sixo. He used to walk thirty miles in order to meet his 'woman', but
his sense of time often left him with only an hour with her before he had to
set off home again. Later in the same section we hear of another of Sixo's
encounters with 'Patsy the Thirty-Mile woman'.

Sethe thinks about the significance of her house, which Paul D had
suggested she leave. She too remembers Sweet Home and the way in
which she used to personalise the kitchen of her owner, Mrs Garner, with
sprigs of flowers and herbs. We learn more about Baby Suggs's eight
children, the nature of their six fathers, and the way in which the dual
systems of slavery and racism affected the lives of black people. The one
child she was allowed to keep was Halle, who worked on Sundays in order
to pay for her freedom. Baby Suggs regards Sethe's attempts to make a
home of Sweet Home with cynicism: 'A bigger fool never lived' (p. 24).
Paul D gazes at Sethe, who, with her eyes shut, seems more manageable.
He remembers how much he and the other Sweet Home men, with the
exception of Sixo, had wanted to be with her. Sethe, conscious of his
glance, remembers that she only used to see her husband in daylight on
Sunday mornings. She recalls her desire for a ceremony when she first
decided to marry Halle. Aged fourteen, she made a dress secretly, after
asking Mrs Garner's permission to get married to Halle.

This section begins with the aftermath of making love, and closes with
the memory of Sethe's first 'coupling' with Halle. They had sex in a corn
field as a gesture of consideration to the other men, but for all their
thoughtfulness, the moving of the corn on a windless day meant that the
observers were perfectly aware of what was taking place. The men feasted
on the broken ears of corn that evening.

NOTES AND GLOSSARY:
the wrought iron on her back: the hard, ridged scars
pay dirt: earth or ore that yields profit to a miner
earth-over: the natural oven that Sixo has made
shirt waist: blouse
salsify: herb with purple flowers
butter wouldn't come: the milk wouldn't turn to butter when churned
bristle: hog's hair for making ink (and paintbrushes)
checkers: a game of draughts
Redmen: American Indians
jailed down ... jailed up: describing the way in which the juice streamed down, and the way in which the same free-flowing juice has been imprisoned. This repetition, with its contrasting connotations of enclosure and freedom, draws attention to a larger scheme of repetition in the passage

ONE   **Section 3   p. 28**

This section contains several layers of narrative, told by different characters and set in different times. The section begins by describing Denver and the 'sweet' and increasingly adult games that she plays by herself in a green bower created by boxwood bushes. During her play she remembers the events of an evening several years ago. After a similar game in the boxwood, involving cologne and nudity, she returned home and saw her mother being embraced by a white dress. She interprets this vision as a sign that the baby ghost has plans. The weather and the sight of Sethe make her remember the story of her own birth, which she loves to tell and to hear told. The narrative switches to Sethe's voice. As she tells the tale of her escape from Sweet Home, she remembers the language and dancing of her own people and the vague relationship that she had with her own mother. We are presented with the image of Sethe staggering through the woods, very pregnant with Denver. Her feet were so swollen and bruised that she could hardly walk. She lay down in the snow and was discovered by Amy Denver, a white girl. Amy was on her way to Boston to buy velvet. Sethe crawled into a lean-to for the night, and Amy massaged her feet. This section is recounted in the present tense. We return to a more recent past. After Denver has told Sethe about the kneeling dress, Sethe tells Denver about Schoolteacher who came to Sweet Home after the death of Mr Garner.

There is a shift to the immediate present of the novel and the progress of the narrative. Paul D has changed 124 Bluestone Road and the lives of its inhabitants. The ghost has gone. Sethe wakes up next to Paul D after their first night together, and remembers Denver's vision of several years before. She wonders about the nature of the 'plans' the baby could have. Paul D sings as he mends the furniture he had broken the day before. He recalls his own past; the prison work he was forced to do in Alfred, Georgia, and the songs he and the other men sang as they worked. He asks Sethe's permission to stay with her and Denver. Sethe is positive, and tells him not to worry about Denver's reaction since she is a charmed child. She tells him of Denver's miraculous birth and attributes Amy's appearance to Denver's destiny. After Schoolteacher came to find them, and Sethe went to prison. Denver was not touched by the rats there although they ate everything else.

NOTES AND GLOSSARY:

wild veronica: a wildflower, Speedwell, with small pink, white or blue and purple flowers

the War Years: the American Civil War (1861–5)

bloody side of the Ohio river: the Ohio separates the state of Ohio from West Virginia and Kentucky. Virginia was one of the eleven states that seceded from the Federal Government. Kentucky was a slave state. Its governors favoured secession but were defeated. Ohio shares northern liberal attitudes, and was urbanised rather than agricultural, as can be seen from Garner's ecstatic praise of Cincinnati's civic development (p. 142). With the Northwest Ordinance of 1787 slavery was prohibited in all territory north of Ohio

mossy teeth: teeth that have become green through not having been cleaned

trash: white trash, i.e. poor whites

pot liquor: liquid left in the pot after cooking meat and/or vegetables

pay for ... passage: this telling detail would suggest that Amy's mother was an immigrant. She too is heading for the freedom of the north, although Boston is much further away than she thinks

foal: give birth like a mare

swole: swollen

bedding dress: bridal attire for the wedding night

lisle: fine cotton thread, a delicate fabric

rememory: a word combining memory, remembrance and the idea of repetition

emerald closet: the enclosure of boxwood

serge: worsted or wool, a much more practical and robust material

molly apple: fruits from the American Molle tree, from which wine can be made

---

ONE **Section 4   p. 43**

Denver is less than happy about the relationship between her mother and Paul D. After three days she asks Paul D how long he intends to 'hang around'. Sethe is embarrassed, while Paul D is wounded. He drops the mug of coffee he is holding and asks if he should leave. Sethe says no and Denver once again is banished from the kitchen. Sethe and Paul D discuss the situation. Sethe apologises for her daughter's behaviour but will not permit Paul D to criticise her. Paul D thinks that Sethe loves too intensely. He tells her that it does not have to be a choice between Denver and himself, and offers his support if she wants to go 'inside' and tackle her buried memories.

At Paul D's suggestion, they decide to go to the carnival. It is Sethe's first outing in eighteen years. Their three shadows appear to be continually holding hands, independent of their actions. Denver is sullen while Paul D is in an infectiously good mood; smiling and talking to everyone who passes. The amusement of the carnival lies in seeing white people making fools of themselves. Denver feels more favourable towards Paul D, and on the way home their shadows are holding hands once again.

NOTES AND GLOSSARY:

croaker sack:	bag made out of heavy cloth, such as burlap
sawyer:	someone who saws wood for a living
barker:	a person who proclaims the attractions and whets the interest of the crowd
Pickaninnies:	a derogatory word for black children
horehound:	minty-tasting herb

ONE **Section 5 p. 51**

A young black woman is waiting for them on a tree stump in front of 124 Bluestone Road when Paul D, Sethe and Denver return from the carnival. She has emerged from the river, and sleeps by the riverside for a day until she finds the strength to walk to 124. Her skin is soft and unlined and she is dressed in expensive clothes. As soon as Sethe sees her face she has to run to the outdoor privy, and, before reaching it, she is forced to urinate outside. The flow reminds her of when her waters broke at Denver's birth. The girl calls herself Beloved. She drinks four cupfuls of water and falls asleep. Denver is fascinated by the new guest. Paul D and Sethe do not press her for the details of her origins. Beloved sleeps for four days, nursed by Denver who is as patient with the invalid as she is irritable with her mother. Her behaviour makes Sethe realise how lonely Denver has been. Denver lies to her mother to protect Beloved, denying that the supposedly sick girl lifted the rocking chair with one hand. Paul D knows that she is lying, and 'if there had been an open latch between them, it had closed'.

NOTES AND GLOSSARY:

sorghum:	a kind of cereal, requiring harvesting
'talking sheets':	scandalous leaflets and newspapers
bluing:	a preparation of blue and violet dyes used to offset the discolouring of white sheets
taffy:	like toffee
lumbar:	the lumbar region is located in the lower back

ONE **Section 6 p. 57**

Beloved is obsessed with Sethe and waits for her to get up in the morning and to come home from work at night. A month has passed since Beloved's arrival. She derives immense satisfaction from hearing about

Sethe's past, and asks her questions that provoke stories. She asks Sethe about the earrings she once wore and Sethe tells the two girls about her wedding with Halle, enlarging upon the details provided in Section 2. She stole pieces of fabric from which to sew a dress, that later she had to unpiece in order to replace them in the places which she had found them. She had wanted some sort of celebration and Mrs Garner, recognising her desires, gave her a pair of crystal earrings as a present. Beloved asks Sethe whether her mother ever braided her hair. Sethe remembers that her mother and the other women spoke another language. She hardly knew her mother, who slept in a different cabin and was at work all day. The woman who nursed her was called Nan. She remembers Nan telling her that she was the only child that her mother claimed as her own. When they were on the boat travelling from Africa to America, Sethe's mother had various unwanted children whom she 'threw away' and did not name. Sethe remembers her mother showing her a branded mark on her ribcage by which she could always recognise her. We learn that Sethe's mother was hanged along with many of the other women on the farm, but that Sethe never found out for what reason. The section finishes with the question that is perplexing Denver. How could Beloved know to ask Sethe about her earrings?

NOTES AND GLOSSARY:

damper:	part of a stove that, when regulated, allows the passage of more or less air to the fire
zealot:	someone fanatical and enthusiastic
rutabaga:	large yellow root vegetable, like a turnip
peck:	a measure of capacity used for dry goods, equivalent to about two gallons
sweet william:	garden flower with large, colourful rosettes
press:	cupboard for clothes
dresser scarf:	runner for the dressing table

ONE   Section 7   p. 64

Another week has passed. Beloved does not speak to Paul D. He perceives her as 'shining' with sexual readiness. After a meal he interrogates her about her family and origins. She seems to be different from the other persecuted black people he has known. He wants her to leave, and just as he is thinking of finding her a place to work in town, Beloved is seized by a choking fit. She and Denver retire, and from then on they sleep in the same room. Denver is very happy with this arrangement. Sethe is remonstrating with Paul D and reminds him of the dangers that beset homeless black women. The subject of Halle comes up, and Sethe reveals her bitterness at his failure to meet up with her in order to escape together.

Paul D tells her that Halle was in the loft and witnessed her rape by Schoolteacher's nephews. The last time that Paul D saw Halle he was sitting by the butter churn with butter all over his face. This is the piece of information which he had decided that she need never know in Section 1. Paul D saw Halle but couldn't speak to him because he had a bit in his mouth. He is the last of the Sweet Home men: 'one crazy, one sold, one missing, one burnt'. He tells Sethe how the sight of a rooster named Mister brought home his own impotence. He realised that it had more identity and freedom than he did although he was a man and the other a bird. Schoolteacher had changed Paul D irrevocably.

NOTES AND GLOSSARY:

diddled: played with

regulators: bands of volunteer committees in the USA who saw their role as to preserve order, prevent crime and administer justice. All too often this justice involved violence and racism

paterollers: patrollers

posses: gangs of white men who roam at night, administering their own brand of justice

Klan: Ku Klux Klan (KKK). A secret organisation originating in southern USA after the Civil War that aimed to maintain white supremacy by violent means

dragon: one of the titles that is awarded to leaders within the KKK is 'Grand Dragon'

clabber: sour milk that has thickened or curdled

peeps: chicks

ONE **Section 8 p. 74**

Beloved dances with Denver. She tells Denver about the place where she was before she came to 124 Bluestone Road. It was hot and full of dead people. She claims that she came back to see Sethe, and remembers playing with Denver in her bower. Denver wants Beloved to promise not to tell Sethe who she really is. In order to appease her she tells the story of her birth, beginning from where the narrative left off in Section 3. She tells of Amy and her desire for velvet and the way she massaged Sethe's feet. Denver feels that the events of the story are happening to her and Sethe's voice takes over the narrative. It was Amy who described the wounds of Sethe's bleeding back as a tree. She dressed Sethe's ravaged back with spider webs and sang to her. She forbade Sethe to die in the night and they settled down to sleep. Amy padded Sethe's misshapen feet with leaves. They arrived at the Ohio river and found a broken boat. Sethe's waters broke and she gave birth to Denver on the banks of the Ohio. Amy helped and together they wrapped the newborn baby in their underwear. Sethe agreed to give it the name of her protector, and Denver is 'christened'.

NOTES AND GLOSSARY:

mossy teeth: on this occasion, means the two nephews of School-teacher

tail: the end of a gust of wind

hankering: can mean strong desire, yearning. Here suggests leaning over

---

ONE **Section 9 p. 86**

Sethe misses Baby Suggs and her calming presence. To pay homage to Halle, whom she now knows must be dead, and to the stirred-up memories of her past, she decides to go to the Clearing, accompanied by the two girls. She describes the way 124 Bluestone Road was as she first knew it, during her twenty-eight days of unslaved life. It was a meeting place, and a place in which people congregated and received messages. Baby Suggs was an unchurched preacher before she took to her bed. Her sermons took place in the Clearing and evoked self-love and respect amongst the members of her black congregation.

There is a flashback to Sethe's past. She remembers waking up on the banks of the Ohio, having given birth to Denver and been deserted by Amy. A man named Stamp Paid helped her to cross the river, where she was met by a woman called Ella. When she arrived for the first time at 124 Bluestone Road, Baby Suggs washed her in sections and treated her wounded back and feet, uncaking the dried milk from her nipples and binding her womb. The next day she was reunited with her three children whom she had sent ahead. The baby girl played with her crystal earrings.

The narrative returns to the present tense. Sethe is in the Clearing with the girls. She asks the spirit of Baby Suggs to massage her neck. At first it obliges, gentle and reassuring, but then the ghostly fingers begin to choke her. Beloved and Denver run to her rescue, and Beloved touches and kisses Sethe's neck, behaving as if she were a baby. At first Sethe thinks that Baby Suggs has tried to kill her, but then she realises that the touch was not that of her mother-in-law. The touch resembled that of the spirit that used to inhabit 124 Bluestone Road and she concludes that it must have retreated to the Clearing after Paul D banished it from the house. For a moment she thinks that the ghostly fingers and Beloved's caresses are one and the same, but she puts the thought out of her mind. She realises that Denver and Beloved behave as if they are sisters, each compensating and fulfilling the needs of the other and showing no competitiveness in their affection to her.

When they get home, Paul D embraces Sethe. We learn that Beloved is jealous of Paul D and of the time that Sethe spends with him. Denver accuses Beloved of being the one to choke her mother. Denver is convinced that Beloved is her sister come back to life. She remembers when she was seven and spent a year going to school at Lady Jones's until a fellow school boy, Nelson Lord, asked her whether it was true that Sethe had murdered her baby sister. When she reported this conversation to her mother she went deaf rather than hear Sethe's answer. She stopped attending the school, and lived in a world cut off from sound for two years. The first thing that she heard was the baby ghost trying to climb the stairs. From that point on the baby was characterised by its spiteful behaviour, the venomous presence that the two women attempt to summon and that is described in the first sentence of the book. Denver has always been the most sensitive and most needful of the ghost's presence, since it was her companion when she was a child. She feels that Beloved is hers and realises that she is prepared to betray Sethe on her behalf. Beloved watches turtles mating, and sees how the female will risk everything for one touch of the male.

NOTES AND GLOSSARY:

AME:	African Methodist Episcopal, an offshoot of Methodism founded in 1787 by Richard Allen, a former slave. In the 1840s there were many female converts to this religion, particularly in Ohio. Women such as Jarena Lee and Julia Foote challenged masculinist mid-century methodism by preaching and travelling without official recognition
leavins:	left-overs
slop for hogs:	used as food for the pigs
revivals:	evangelist church unions and festivals that take place out of doors
buckeyes:	horse chestnuts
flatbed:	flatboat or flat-bottomed boat
cardinal:	a bird with a red crest
four o'clocks:	a plant whose flowers need sunlight and only open late in the afternoon

---

ONE   **Section 10**   **p. 106**

Paul D tells us in the present tense of his experiences in the prison camp in Alfred, Georgia. He was sent there after he attempted to kill Brandywine, the man to whom Schoolteacher sold him after the break-up of Sweet Home. He was one of forty-six men who worked in a chain gang. They lived in wooden boxes set in a ditch. In the morning each man was linked to the others by a length of chain, and the white guards selected men at random to perform fellatio on them. During the day the men worked together, singing as they swung their sledge hammers. Paul D had been there for eighty-six days when it began to rain and after nine days of downpour they were compelled to stop working. They were left chained up inside their boxes. It rained so hard that the mud roofs began to cave in. The men escaped by diving underneath the iron bars that formed one side of their boxes. The fact that they were all linked by the chain meant that each and every one was brought to salvation. They found themselves with an exiled and sick band of Cherokee Indians, who fed them and helped them remove the chains. Paul D asked their advice as to how he could get to the North and they told him to follow the blossom on the trees. He followed their advice, and on the way he spent a year and a half in Delaware with a 'weaver lady'.

NOTES AND GLOSSARY:

buckboard:	open carriage
coffle:	a group of slaves chained together for travelling
feldspar:	any aluminium silicate. Can be flesh-red, bluish or greenish. Here it refers to a feldspar quarry
bay:	to cry or shout. The word has bestial associations
cottonmouths:	a venomous water snake that flourishes in ditches, called so because of the white interior of its mouth
unshriven dead:	someone who has not been given absolution before death
redbud trees:	Judas trees; bushy trees with pink or red flowers
Cherokee:	a tribe of native Americans who originally numbered 45,000. They formerly possessed large tracts of land. They sided with the English in most disputes between European colonists and with the Royalist party in the Revolutionary War. With the increasing number of white settlers they were dispossessed of most of their land
for whom a rose was named:	the Cherokee rose (*rosa laevigata*) is a Chinese climbing rose with a fragrant white blossom
Oklahoma:	those who had not moved were driven to the north eastern corner of Oklahoma
George III:	(1738–1820) King of England 1760–1811, during Britain's War of Independence with the USA
published as a newspaper:	Elias Boudinot edited *The Cherokee Phoenix* (1828–35), the first newspaper for an Indian tribe
Oglethorpe:	(1697–1785) the founder of the state of Georgia
Andrew Jackson:	(1767–1845) the seventh president of the USA. When America and Great Britain went to war in 1812 the Creek Indians staged their own attack on the

Americans, Jackson was the general in charge of the Tennessee troops

wrote their language: the Cherokee written alphabet of eighty-five characters was invented in 1821 by George Guess, also known as Sequoyah

barnacles: pincers placed in a horse's nostrils to prevent it moving while being shod

Free North: the Northern States opposed the Confederate States on many issues. One of these was slavery

---

ONE **Section 11 p. 114**

Paul D stops sleeping with Sethe at night. At first he sleeps in the rocking chair, then in Baby Suggs's room, then in the storeroom and finally in the cold house. He realises that it is not any discontent on his own part but that he is being moved by someone else, who has prevented him from being with Sethe. One night Beloved comes to visit him in the coldroom. She lifts her skirts and asks him to touch her 'on the inside part'. He remonstrates with her, reminding her of how much Sethe loves her, but Beloved persists in her desire to be touched and called by name. Finally Paul D succumbs and finds himself saying, over and over again 'Red heart. Red heart. Red heart.'

NOTES AND GLOSSARY:

Lot's wife: Lot's wife was turned to a pillar of salt when she looked back as she and her husband fled from Sodom (see the Bible, Genesis 19, 1–26)

ONE **Section 12 p. 118**

Denver is convinced that Beloved is her sister. She is very careful not to press her for information, for fear that Beloved might leave and she be left alone once more. Sethe questions Beloved about her background and her clothing, and confesses her suspicions to Denver. Denver refrains from agreeing with her mother. She loves being looked at by Beloved, and thinks of tasks and ways in which they might be prolonged in order to occupy the mysterious guest. One day the two girls go into the cold house in order to get the cider jug. Beloved disappears. Denver is desperate. Her source of life has disappeared. After some time Beloved comes back. She explains to Denver that she does not want to return to the other place: 'This is the place I am.'

NOTES AND GLOSSARY:

shoot: an exclamation of surprise or annoyance

ONE   **Section 13   p. 125**

Paul D feels that he is being forced into having sex with Beloved. His powerlessness makes him question his manhood. When he was at Sweet Home, Mr Garner prided himself that Paul D and the other slaves were men. Now Paul D wonders whether he is a man, or whether it was only a definition. He decided to tell Sethe in the hopes that she will help him. He goes to meet her after work, and instead of admitting his weakness, he finds himself asking her if she will have his child. It seems the solution to his problems. She laughs, and says she is too old. It starts snowing and Paul D carries Sethe on his back. They are happy and so absorbed in each other that they are surprised to see Beloved who has come to meet Sethe. The perfect moment is interrupted. That evening Sethe invites Paul D to sleep in her room, undoing Beloved's power to make him sleep in the cold house. Paul D remembers the last time he had been grateful to a woman. When he arrived in Delaware the weaver-lady gave him a meal and a bed to sleep in for the first time in his life. Sethe lies next to him and thinks that he is jealous of her existing daughters, and that is why he wants to have his own child. She too, like Denver, is beginning to think of Beloved as the baby girl come back to life.

NOTES AND GLOSSARY:

steer bulls:	bulls castrated before sexual maturity
shucking:	corn husks
cobs:	small stacks of grain or hay

ONE   **Section 14   p. 133**

Denver warns Beloved that Sethe might object if she causes Paul D to go away. Beloved is not listening and pulls a wisdom tooth out of her mouth. She thinks that it is only a matter of time before she explodes into her various components. She cries in the kitchen, holding the tooth in her hand. It is snowing outside.

ONE   **Section 15   p. 135**

This section refers to the period preceding Sethe's drastic act in the woodshed. It is told in the present tense. Stamp Paid had collected two bucketsful of blackberries and brought them to 124 Bluestone Road. Baby Suggs decided to make some pies, and to invite a few neighbours. The project for the feast grows and grows, and that evening the house hosted and fed almost ninety people. The next day Baby Suggs sensed disapproval in the air. She was in the garden while Stamp Paid chopped wood. She realised that she had exaggerated, breaking her own rule of 'Good is knowing when to stop' (p. 87). Her display of bounty had irritated their guests. Behind the smell of disapproval and envy she discerned something else, 'dark and coming'. As she wondered what it could be, we learn about her life on Sweet Home. She was bought by Mr Garner with her ten-year-old son Halle. She cost relatively little because she had a broken hip. Sweet Home was small compared to other places she had been, and her job consisted of assisting Mrs Garner with the household chores. Her hip caused her pain, and, after ten years, Halle decided to pay for her freedom with his own labour. At first she agreed only to make him happy, but when she arrived in Cincinnati with Mr Garner she realised that he was right, and that there was 'nothing like freedom in the world'. She noticed her hands and the sound of her heart beating for the first time. We learn the reason why the Garners had always called her Jenny. It was the name on her bill of sale. She decided to keep the name of Baby Suggs in the hopes that she will be found by the man she had claimed as husband, and who had given her the name of Baby and his name, Suggs. They went to visit Garner's friends, the Bodwins. The sister and brother were both against slavery. They had found a house for Baby and suggested that she could do washing and mend shoes for a living. Baby Suggs had imagined that she might be able to reunite her family. Of her eight children, she had a little information about the whereabouts of each. She knew that two were dead, but hoped to be able to contact four of the others. After two years of effort she realised that it was impossible. She contented herself with Halle, and the news that he was married and that Sethe was pregnant.

During this reminiscence, Baby Suggs had remained immobile in the garden. She regretted the munificence of the feast. She felt the disapproval of her neighbours and saw the image of a pair of high-topped shoes.

NOTES AND GLOSSARY:
hominy: prepared corn
gone to Glory: died

ONE **Section 16 p. 148**

This passage relates the events leading up to Sethe's murder of her baby daughter. Once again the present tense is used. Schoolteacher, with one of his nephews, the sheriff and a slave catcher drove up to 124 Bluestone Road to take back Sethe and her children in order to restock Sweet Home. They went round to the back of the house and found Stamp Paid and Baby Suggs in the garden. Sethe was in the woodshed. She had cut her toddler's throat with a handsaw and had attempted to do the same to Howard and Buglar. She was in the process of trying to smash three-week-old Denver's head against the wall planks. For a moment we hear Schoolteacher's thoughts. He refers to Sethe as if she were an animal, gone wild because of having been overbeaten. He regarded this as a pity since she has ten breeding years left. Schoolteacher's nephew was shaking, unable to understand why Sethe had committed such an awful action.

Baby Suggs came into the woodshed and immediately nursed Howard and Buglar. Sethe would not relinquish her dead toddler. Baby Suggs told her to feed Denver, and insisted that she hold only one baby at a time. Sethe fed Denver with a nipple covered with the blood of her sister. Sethe and Denver were taken away in a cart. A crowd of neighbours was there to watch, and they hummed as she left. Baby Suggs was wishing that she had kept Denver, when two white children came and brought her a pair of high-topped shoes to mend.

NOTES AND GLOSSARY:

coons: derogatory word for black people

ONE   **Section 17   p. 154**

The narrative returns to the present of the novel. Stamp Paid takes Paul D aside and shows him a newspaper cutting about Sethe. Paul D cannot read, but gazes at the picture, and tells Stamp that it cannot be Sethe because the mouth is drawn wrongly. He looks at the picture with a sense of trepidation. Black people rarely appeared in newspapers unless involved with some kind of crime or atrocity. Stamp tries to explain the events that have just been told in the last section. He describes the difficulty of procuring the blackberries, and explains why he and Baby had been looking in the wrong direction the following day. He believes that nobody warned them of the approach of the white men, with the 'righteous Look' because they were disgruntled after the excesses of the feast the night before. Paul D keeps interrupting him to say that the picture is not of Sethe. Stamp gives up on his own account of events, and reads the newspaper article to Paul D. Paul D still does not believe it can have been Sethe.

ONE   **Section 18   p. 159**

Paul D has shown Sethe the newspaper clipping, hoping that the two of them will be able to laugh at the mix-up and at Stamp's interference. Sethe tries to tell him her account of events. She circles around the subject. She tells him how surprised she was to find the baby girl crawling already when she arrived at 124 Bluestone Road. She explains that, without female company or advice at Sweet Home, she was never quite sure how to tend to her children. She tells him how proud she was to have escaped from Sweet Home on her own. Her stolen freedom brought with it the power to love. She realised that her children must never live the kind of life she lived on Sweet Home. When she recognised Schoolteacher's hat she knew that she had to protect her children. By killing them she foiled School-teacher's plans and she sent them to safety. Paul D is scared by the way Sethe explains her actions. As far as he is concerned her love is 'too thick'. He challenges her solution, and reminds her that, despite her efforts, Howard and Buglar are as good as lost, while Denver is timid and the baby girl is dead. He judges her, and tells her that she is a human being, and not a beast: 'You got two feet, Sethe, not four.' He does not say goodbye but takes his hat, and leaves, saying he will be back late.

NOTES AND GLOSSARY:

sassafras:	dried root bark from which antiseptic oil, including camphor, is obtained
Comfrey:	herb with soothing properties
heft:	weight, substance

TWO   **Section 1   p. 169**

A year has passed since the time in which the novel began. 124 Bluestone Road is resounding with the voices of black women. Stamp Paid goes to the front door. He wants to apologise to Sethe for the lack of consideration he has shown her as Baby Suggs's 'kin'. He regrets his readiness to show Paul D the newspaper clipping. He has since realised that he may have denied Sethe her chance of happiness, and Denver the presence of a normal man in her home. The last time he visited the house was on the occasion of Baby Suggs's funeral. The neighbours attended out of respect to the dead woman, but refused to eat the food that Sethe had prepared. Stamp is not successful in making his planned visit. He is not accus-tomed to knocking on doors since his benevolent acts have earned him the privilege of entering unannounced. The necessary formality of his visit prevents him from carrying out his intentions. He remembers the former anger he felt towards Baby Suggs when she gave up her religious duties and devoted the remainder of her life to the contemplation of colour. Now he begins to understand why she lost her faith and her will to participate. He remembers a conversation that they had. She tells him that despite her belief in God and her freedom, the white men nevertheless intruded into her private familial space: 'they came in my yard'.

Sethe tries to forget the unpleasant turn her life has taken. She takes the two girls ice-skating. They have three skates between them. They fall and laugh, and come home to a change of clothes and hot sweet milk. They are sitting in front of the fire when Sethe realises that Beloved must be her daughter. Beloved is humming a song that Sethe invented and sang to her children. There is no other way that she could know it unless she is Sethe's missing daughter. Despite the implications of this knowledge

Sethe remains completely calm, and leaves the girls to sleep in front of the fire. The next morning she cooks breakfast for the girls and is late for work. She now thinks that the shadows holding hands on the day of the carnival represented herself and her two daughters. She is full of hope that her sons too might return. She desires nothing other than what is in her house. On the way to work she is excited by the idea that she will no longer have to explain or remember the events of the past. She makes a mental list of all the things that she can now forget and in the process she describes her stay in prison and her attendance at the baby's funeral.

When Stamp overcomes his pride, and knocks at the door of 124 Bluestone Road, Sethe is at work. He sees Beloved and Denver through the window. They do not respond to his knock. He goes to see Ella, the woman who met Sethe on the other side of the Ohio and took her to 124 for the first time. He asks her if she knows who the strange woman at the house could be. She does not know but tells him that Paul D is sleeping in the church cellar. He is astonished that the community of black people could let one of their number sleep in the cold without offering him a place in which to stay. Ella is wary of Paul D because of his association with Sethe. She has never been convinced that Sethe was Halle's wife, or that her children were really Baby Suggs's grandchildren. Stamp explains that Paul D and Sethe knew each other at Sweet Home, and that Paul D left Sethe after hearing about the murder she committed. It seems that this information changes Ella's attitude to Paul D.

At work Sethe ignores the reproaches of her employer. She is angry with 'whitefolks' and no longer makes any distinction between those who sought to help her, like the Bodwins or Amy, and those who perpetrate the innumerable evils against black people. Her mind is flooded with Sweet Home memories. The thought of Beloved at home makes her conscious of all the things from which she has succeeded in saving her children. She remembers Schoolteacher measuring her with string, and making two lists to compare her human and animal characteristics. She thinks of her work on the farm, and her laughing sons and baby daughter. She recalls the realisation that her sons too would have to work, and that Halle, made to work full-time on Sweet Farm, was denied the possibility of purchasing freedom for himself or his family.

NOTES AND GLOSSARY:

Fugitive Bill: a series of Fugitive Slave Laws were passed to protect the property rights of slave-owners. These laws imposed severe penalties on runaway slaves. The Fugitive Slave Act of 1793 was strengthened in 1850. It is to this later legislation that Sethe refers

manumission: formal emancipation from slavery

Dred Scott: Dred Scott was a slave who married and had two children while on free soil, but he and his family were later taken back to Missouri. In 1846 he sued for his freedom. The supreme court of Missouri held that his return meant that he was a slave and had no standing in the court whereas the USA circuit court decided that, while still a slave, he had standing in the court as a citizen. The case was argued by the supreme court and the decision was taken (not unanimous) that Scott was not a citizen. This ruling denied the rights of congress to make slaves or their descendants citizens, and made it clear that slavery would not be abolished along constitutional lines. Chief Justice Taney who presided over the case virtually announced that as a black slave, Scott had no rights that white men were bound to respect

Sojourner's high-wheeled buggy: Sojourner Truth (?1797–1883) was a female slave. Legally freed, her 'Narrative', transcribed by friends, was published in two versions in 1850 and 1875. She campaigned against tobacco, fashionable dress, alcohol and the segregation of street cars. She fought for evangelism, black people and women's rights

North Star: an anti-slavery newspaper (1847–64) founded in Rochester, New York. It favoured peaceful political methods

bed life: a life of sexual activity for Sethe

taters: potatoes

head cheese: the meat of the head, feet and sometimes of the tongue and heart of a pig cut up finely and seasoned and boiled. This mixture was made into a large sausage or pressed into a thin jellied mass

shoat: a young pig of either sex

would a: would have. Morrison is using colloquial speech to represent Sethe's frantic thought patterns

train: this is probably a reference to the Underground Railroad, a secret network that existed before the Civil War. Fugitive slaves were given clothes and food and helped to escape. Harriet Tubman was one of the most famous black agents. It is significant that Morrison chooses to represent a female conductor (pp. 198, 202) since by this action she commemorates the role of women in the organisation of the Railroad

long-school: people who have studied

TWO   Section 2   p. 200

Sethe's thoughts, unspeakable and unspoken, are conveyed in fragments. She is proud that Beloved has come back to her. She justifies her behaviour by remembering the horrors that would have awaited her children in Sweet Home. She recalls her own relationship with her mother, whom she scarcely saw, and her relationship with Mrs Garner, whom she nursed. She plans her new life with her daughter back from the dead. For the first time since the pink of the baby's gravestone she is noticing colours, and she dwells on all the things she will be able to show and explain to Beloved. She blames Paul D for obscuring the facts that indicated Beloved's identity. Without his presence she is sure that she would have noticed earlier the scratches on Beloved's forehead that correspond to the marks of her fingernails and would have recognised the implications of the way in which her waters seemed to break when she was involuntarily forced to urinate on seeing her daughter. She thinks that she would have questioned the way in which Beloved knew to ask about the crystal earrings, or connected their physical similarities.

NOTES AND GLOSSARY:
holler: shout
spigot: tap

TWO   Section 3   p. 205

Sethe's thoughts are followed by a similar monologue from Denver. She claims Beloved as her sister. Her memory of her loneliness as a child, her only company the ghost, is followed by a description of her fear of her mother. Howard and Buglar used to frighten her, and she lived with the apprehension that that which made it appropriate for her mother to kill her own children might happen again. She used to dream that her mother decapitated her every night and feels that she has to protect Beloved from her mother. The half-hidden memories of the rats and the time she spent in prison return to her. She is convinced that Halle, her 'daddy' will return. She has spent her childhood waiting for him, and hoarding the stories that Baby Suggs used to recount about her favourite son. Denver dreams of being united with her father and of living with him and Beloved. Sethe is denied a place in this dream scenario.

TWO   Section 4   p. 210

Beloved's thoughts are narrated with a technique known as 'stream of consciousness'. These thoughts are even more disjointed than those of her sister and of her mother. She too remembers the grape arbor that Sethe has described, but then goes on to recount the time she spent with the dead. She tells of what seems to be a sea-voyage. This can be read as the story of the slaves who came to America from Africa: the mouldy bread, chains around people's necks, cramped conditions and segregation of the sexes. The entire passage is highly impressionistic but finishes by chronicling Beloved's birth into the world, recounted in Section 5 of Part One of the novel. Just as Sethe sees Beloved as hers, Beloved claims her mother as her own. They are the same person, and the syntactical confusion does much to convey this blurring of personal boundaries: 'she is my face smiling at me'.

TWO   Section 5   p. 214

A more coherent version of Beloved's thoughts is presented. An exchange between Sethe and Beloved is related in the form of a series of questions and answers. Sethe asks her daughter if she has forgiven her and promises to protect her. A similar exchange between Denver and Beloved takes place. Denver too offers to protect Beloved, and warns her against Sethe. The three female voices join together in a chorus. The voice that we associate with Beloved is increasingly resentful. She accuses Sethe of leaving her, of not smiling and of hurting her. They reiterate the fact that they all belong to each other.

TWO   Section 6   p. 218

Paul D is sitting on the church steps, drinking whisky and abandoning himself to the thoughts of his past. He describes the plan that they had made to escape from Sweet Home, which was later complicated by several factors, namely Halle's new working arrangements, the increasing demands of Mrs Garner, Sethe's pregnancy and the fact that Sixo was kept tied up at night. Once again he questions his manhood, and wonders whether it is merely a word conferred upon him by Mr Garner. He remembers the confusion that befell their attempted escape. He was separated from his brothers, and he and Sixo were caught by School-teacher. The white men discussed the price that he would fetch on the slave market. Sixo retaliated and the white men tried to set fire to him. The wood was wet and Sixo laughed and sang. They shot him. His last triumphant shout was 'Seven-O.' The Thirty-Mile-Woman had escaped and was pregnant with his child. Paul D remembers how he was shackled and wearing a neck collar when Sethe came to see him to ask about Halle. She had already sent her children away. This is the scene that Paul D remembered in the first section. It preceded her violation and the beating she received in the barn.

NOTES AND GLOSSARY:

dray:	a kind of cart
a pitching game:	a game involving throwing
dry-goods church:	the church's premises had once been a shop
tackroom:	room for storing horses' harnesses
doggone:	(*exclamation*) damned
juba:	rhythmic African dancing and singing
buckboard:	open horse-drawn carriage

TWO   **Section 7   p. 230**

Stamp Paid finds Paul D on the church steps, and apologises to him for the nights that he has spent there, offering him the use of any coloured person's house in the neighbourhood. He offers to rectify any damage he has caused. He tells Paul D how he got his name. Before choosing the name of Stamp Paid, he was called Joshua. The man for whom he worked took his wife, Vashti, for his own sexual purposes. Stamp thought about killing his owner and also his wife. In the end they escaped and he renamed himself. Stamp tries to explain Sethe's motives when she killed her daughter. Paul D tells him about Beloved, and asks him, overcome by the misery of their lives: 'How much is a nigger supposed to take?'

THREE   **Section 1   p. 239**

The situation in 124 Bluestone Road has degenerated. Sethe has stopped going to work, and is getting more and more emaciated, while Beloved swells in size. Denver is excluded from their games and struggles for power. Beloved blackmails Sethe, reminding her of what she did, and Sethe serves her daughter. Denver's allegiance changes: she moves from wanting to protect Beloved to fearing for the safety of her mother. Sethe becomes ill and Denver realises that she is the one who will have to leave the house and do something in order to save the situation. She is frightened at the thought of this, but she hears the voice of Baby Suggs, and plucks up the courage to call on Lady Jones at the house in which she used to receive lessons. Denver asks for help, and from then on she begins to find gifts of food in the woods near her home. Scraps of paper are attached indicating the owner of the dishes or the donor of the present. She goes to thank her neighbours and in this way becomes reintegrated with the world outside the house. She hears people talk about the happy times they enjoyed at 124. Meanwhile the situation within the house is deteriorating rapidly. Sethe and Beloved have swapped roles, and Sethe is becoming as weak as a baby. Denver realises that Beloved is making Sethe pay for her actions, while Sethe is trying to compensate for what she did. Beloved is the only person whom she feels she has to convince. Denver has become completely insignificant in the stalemate, and realises that she has to go out to look for work. She goes to see the Bodwins in the hope that they will help the third generation in the way that they helped both Baby Suggs and her mother. In exchange for information about the reality of her home life, the woman who works there, Janey, agrees to help Denver to get work with the Bodwins. She suggests that Denver stay there at night. Janey tells all the other neighbours that Sethe's dead daughter has come back to haunt her, inflating Denver's reserved account. Ella hears this tale and determines to come to Sethe's rescue.

As Denver is sitting waiting for Mr Bodwin to come and pick her up for her first night at work, thirty women come to 124 Bluestone Road. They pray and sing.

As he drives the cart, Mr Bodwin, now seventy years old, thinks of the house in which he was born and recalls the time when he was an active abolitionist, working against the evils of slavery.

The women gathered about 124 Bluestone Road see Sethe and Beloved in the yard. Sethe is breaking ice into chunks. Beloved is naked, glistening and swollen like a pregnant woman. Sethe looks up and sees the approach of Mr Bodwin. She feels the hummingbirds in her hair, and sees a white man coming into her yard. Still holding the ice-pick she runs out of the yard, determined to protect her daughters.

NOTES AND GLOSSARY:

She was wild game: Beloved is unpredictable. She does not abide by societal or familial rules

rout: Baby Suggs uses this word to imply the utter impossibility of any kind of struggle between black and white people, when the latter possess all the power and resources

chippy: prostitute, sexually promiscuous woman

Settlement Fee: the fee for being allowed to take up residence

junked: shunned her socially. Other than nodding at Sethe at the carnival section, Ella had not spoken to Sethe in eighteen years

Cobbler: an iced drink made from wine, sugar and fruit juice

harps: Jews' harps – musical instruments played like a mouth organ

brake ... bell: instruments used to restrain slaves

the Society: a reference to the American Anti-Slavery Society, formed in 1833 in Philadelphia

the Secessionists: those states that decided to withdraw from the Union, that is, the rebel or Confederate States

THREE   Section 2   p. 263

Beloved has gone. Some people say that she just disappeared, while others claim that she exploded in front of their eyes. Paul D is convinced of her departure because the dog, Here Boy, has returned to the house. Mr Bodwin is trying to sell the house: it transpires that Sethe tried to stab Mr Bodwin with the ice-pick, and was prevented by Ella hitting her. Mr Bodwin saw Beloved, but the women deny her existence. Paul D and Stamp agree that he must also have seen that Sethe was trying to reach him, but, luckily, he chose not to acknowledge it.

The next day Paul D sees Denver. She is thinner and looks very much like Halle. Her answers to Paul D are civil and she seems to have grown up. Miss Bodwin had been teaching her and she is looking for an afternoon job in order to supplement her wages and support her mother. Paul D asks her if she thinks that Beloved was her sister, and she does not answer him directly. She tells him to be careful of the way in which he treats Sethe. Paul D remembers his attempted escapes and the various ways in which he was frustrated. He recalls the freedom he experienced in Trenton and the first money that he earned. He goes to 124 Bluestone Road to look for Sethe. She is lying in Baby Suggs's bed singing to herself. Paul D is angry to see her without strength, and realises that she has given up in the way that Baby Suggs did. He tells her that he is going to look after her, and starts by washing her. She looks at him and cries. Beloved, her 'best thing' has left her. He tells her that she herself is her best thing, and that they ought to stay together.

NOTES AND GLOSSARY:

Oberlin: Oberlin College was founded before the Civil War in 1833. It was the first college in the States to adopt coeducation, and in 1835 it admitted students 'without respect to color'. It was a noted centre for anti-slavery sentiments

Rebellers: another word for the Confederate states

Confederate: the name adopted by those states that seceded and formed an independent union at the end of 1860 and the beginning of 1861. The Civil War was their fight against the Federate Government of the North

Yankee: a Union soldier during the Civil War

Union: the Union was the name given to the Northern States

skiff: a light rowing boat

THREE   Section 3   p. 274

An epilogue in the third person describes the way in which Beloved and

the memory of her passed from the protagonist's lives. The novel finishes
with her name.

NOTES AND GLOSSARY:

Disremembered: a word coined by Morrison to imply 'forgotten'. The
prefix 'dis' makes it seem like a deliberate activity:
a conscious choice to *not* remember. This is quite
different from the unconscious process with which
we usually associate 'forgetting'

to pass on: this has a double meaning: 'to retell' or 'to skip'

Part 3

Commentary

The characters

Sethe

Sethe is a pivotal character in *Beloved*. The narrative voice of the novel is most often hers as she relives and 'rememories' the facts of her life as a slave. This awfulness of her life leads her to commit the incomprehensible act in the woodshed: killing her daughter and attempting to kill her two sons in order to prevent them from the suffering that she had experienced.

She rarely saw her mother, and was brought up by a one-armed woman named Nan, while her mother worked in the fields (pp. 30, 60) as a slave. Her mother took her aside one day to show her a mark which was branded on to her ribcage. Later Sethe find her mother hanged, along with many of the other women, but she never discovers the reason for her death. We can assume that Sethe is a second-generation slave, since she can remember her mother speaking another language (p. 62) and being told of her repeated rapes during the voyage to America. Sethe's memories of her youth are vague, but at the age of thirteen she is sold to Sweet Home, a farm in Kentucky. She is bought in order to replace Baby Suggs, whose son she later marries and to whose home she escapes.

While Sweet Home is run by Mr Garner and his wife, Sethe lives in relative tranquillity. She works in the kitchen and makes ink for Mr Garner. All five of the male slaves would like her as a partner, but after a year she chooses Halle to be her husband. They make love in a cornfield in order to spare the feelings of the other slaves, but the waving of the corn on a windless day signals their activity to the watching men. She gets pregnant every year and has three children, two boys named Howard and Buglar, and a baby girl. She is nineteen and pregnant for the fourth time when Mr Garner dies.

His brother-in-law (Schoolteacher) comes to take control of the farm. From this point onwards life becomes unbearable for the slaves. They decide to escape, but in the ensuing confusion Sethe is forced to send her three children on ahead to Baby Suggs's house. After being beaten mercilessly by the nephews, and having to endure the indignity of their sucking milk from her swollen breasts, she runs away on foot. She gives birth to her fourth child with the help of a white girl named Amy, and is helped to cross the Ohio river, in order to reach 124 Bluestone Road where her mother-in-law, Baby Suggs, is living. For twenty-eight days she enjoys freed life before Schoolteacher arrives to take her and her children back to Sweet Home. Rather than let this happen, she takes her children into the woodshed and tries to kill them all in order to preserve them from a life of hopeless slavery.

The intolerable nature of her life is no different to that of many of the other black characters in the novel. The difference lies in her dramatic response. Various characters in the novel try to dissuade her from loving too much (pp. 45, 92). Paul D describes her love as 'too thick', and recognises that to love in such a way is 'risky' given the precarious nature of slave existence (p. 45). Nevertheless, her daughter Denver and the spirit of her dead baby, Beloved, become the focus of her life: she will not allow Paul D to criticise them, and she gives up the responsibility of employment, centring her world within the walls of 124 Bluestone Road. She succeeds in despatching her best thing – her small daughter – to safety by cutting her throat with a handsaw. She sees this act as one of protection and provision for her young but, paradoxically, it proves to be an act of destruction, lending gruesome irony to the phrase, 'mother love was a killer' (p. 132).

Sethe is an impressively strong character. Her determination manifests itself in her successful escape from Sweet Home. Pregnant and wounded she manages to make her way through the woods and across the Ohio river. Although haunted by her memories of the past, she withstands the humiliation of being sexually abused by two men. Halle witnesses this and loses his reason. He is last seen beside the butter churn, spreading butter on his face. She thinks for a moment that it would have been a release if she too could have joined him, but her three children on the way to Ohio needed her and 'no butter play would change that' (p. 71). Sethe's strength is embodied in her remarkable eyes and unflinching gaze. This is the quality that Denver accepts as intrinsic to her mother: Sethe does not look away from a variety of ghastly sights (p. 12). Paul D is similarly struck by her 'polished' eyes (p. 25). When she is on the verge of leaving Sweet Home, she kneels by Paul D and the fire, and he notices the complete absence of expression in her face. Schoolteacher thinks that she looks blind when he sees her in the woodshed (p. 151).

Until Beloved's carnal appearance, Sethe copes with the guilt of her own act and co-habits with her baby daughter's spirit. However, for all her strength, Sethe is beaten by Beloved. She is punished and allows herself to be swamped by her guilt. Mother and daughter become involved in a terrible deadlock of love. Nevertheless, the final exorcism of Beloved and the return of Paul D seem to imply the possibility of a future and Denver is instrumental in reintroducing Sethe into the community from which she has been an exile. Her last words, 'Me? Me?' (p. 273) promise a new life for Sethe in which she, absolved of her guilt, can value herself as her own best thing.

Beloved

Beloved is Sethe's executed daughter come back to life. She is willed into existence by the women of 124 Bluestone Road. Sethe announces ominously that if her daughter would only come back she would be able to explain her actions to her (p. 4). Denver craves companionship and treasures her sister's presence, both ghostly and actual. But Denver is to learn that she is of little importance to Beloved. After the departure of Paul D, Beloved and Sethe engage in a tug of love, guilt and retribution. Beloved lacks the ability to forgive her mother for her crime, echoing Sethe's own inability to forgive herself.

Although Beloved arrives at 124 Bluestone Road as an adult, we witness her living through the human life cycle. At first her needs are for oral gratification and her mother's gaze. She is unable to bear the weight of her own head, and cannot walk or talk properly. At this point she is developmentally and emotionally an infant. She remains at the stage of primary identification, refusing to differentiate herself from her mother: 'her face is my own' (p. 210). During her stay she becomes a vindictive and unrelenting teenager, untouched by the usual rules that regulate a parent–child relationship. Beloved takes emotional advantage of Denver by befriending her, and physical advantage of Paul D by seducing him. She becomes Sethe's judge and begins to take her over. She wears her clothes, imitates her, and laughs 'her laugh' (p. 241). Denver begins to have difficulty in telling them apart, as Beloved dominates Sethe, swelling in size as her mother shrinks. A physical embodiment of the spiteful poltergeist, Beloved is a malignant presence, who would as soon strangle Sethe as soothe her.

Crucially absent from the text is any explanation by the author of why Beloved appears, or where she goes after her disappearance. The novel presents the reaction of others to her presence; by the epilogue she is forgotten. Not one of the characters can remember anything that she said, and it is posited that perhaps she only said and thought what they themselves were thinking (p. 274). This allows a psychoanalytical reading of Beloved's presence: as the incarnation of Sethe's sense of guilt and her unforgiving memory, with which she has to come to terms before she can accept the future that Paul D offers. Beloved can also be seen as America's past of slavery, haunting the reader in the same way as it haunted Toni Morrison herself before she embarked on the novel that took her six years to write. Although Beloved's presence is a negative one, it purges the guilt-ridden Sethe, who needs punishment in order to gain redemption. Denver recounts the way in which her mother seems to provoke Beloved's outrages (p. 252), with a masochistic desire for penance. By choosing to dwell on a period that is embarrassing for America, the novel has a similar cathartic effect on the reader. However, in the epilogue, Toni Morrison repeats that the story 'is not a story to pass on' (p. 275). Paradoxically this is exactly what she, as an author, has done. The double sense of the phrase: to retell, or to skip, reminds readers that the terrible events of slavery must never be forgotten.

Denver

In many ways Denver is a minor character in the novel. She is without a past, excluded from the shared pain of the older protagonists. Her birth is something that happened to Sethe and, although Denver loves the story, when she tells it she switches from a third person narrative to experiencing it as Sethe. Her narrative is overpowered by the past and her voice is drowned. So much of the novel depends on the life at Sweet Home, its dissolution and consequences, that Denver is set aside. She herself is aware of the bond that unites Paul D and her mother and resents it ferociously.

Denver is the character most sensitive to Beloved and her true identity. She drank her sister's blood along with Sethe's milk (p. 152), much to Baby Suggs's horror. As a child, as 'lonely and rebuked' as she claims that the ghost is (p. 13), she plays with Beloved, and her deafness is broken by the sound of the baby girl trying to crawl up the steps. She needs Beloved in the same way that Beloved needs Sethe, and we witness her desolation when Beloved disappears in the coldhouse (pp. 122–3). She feels that she has lost her self, and it is only when she takes responsibility for her own life at the instigation of Nelson Lord that she realises she has a self of her own 'to look out for and preserve' (p. 252).

In many ways, the advent of Beloved is a catalyst for a development in Denver's character and way of living. Nursing their sick guest makes her become patient, while her desire to capture Beloved's attention and divert her makes her become dutiful in the house, inventing chores to do together in order to pass the time. In the deadlock of love in which Beloved and Sethe finally become involved, Denver realises that she is of no importance. Originally prepared to protect Beloved from her saw-wielding mother, she now realises that she must save her mother from Beloved. She reacts, not with the sullen resentment she feels when Paul D arrives, but as an adult. She is forced to leave the yard and find work. When Paul D meets her in the penultimate section of the novel she is composed and mature. She is searching for a second job, and treats, and is treated by, Paul D as a fellow adult. Finally she is successful in breaking out of the narrowly defined, self-destructive circle of family relationships in 124 Bluestone Road.

Paul D

In the penultimate section, Paul D tells Sethe that 'we got more yesterday than anybody'(p. 273). Together with Sethe, Paul D provides the details of oppression and suffering that are the context and justification for Sethe's dramatic gesture in the woodshed. The description of his past prompts some of the more historically allusive passages in Toni Morrison's novel: his experience in the Civil war, travel to the North and time spent at the prison camp. Paul D's narrative voice gives the reader the chilling details of Sixo's death, the humiliation of 'neck jewellery' and of white domination, until the reader is forced to echo his desperate words on the church steps: 'How much is a nigger supposed to take?' (p. 235).

After the break-up of Sweet Home, he attempted to kill his new owner, and was taken to a prison camp. He managed to escape, along with the other members of the chain gang, and they found themselves in a camp of Cherokee Indians. He was the last of the men to leave the Cherokee camp. He goes North, fights on both sides of the Civil War, and spends three years in Delaware with a weaver woman. He envies extended families, having been denied roots by the system of slavery. The same system undermines his sense of manhood so that he feels dispossessed. Although he loves the land and is moved by its texture, he is fully aware that he has no right to it (p. 221).

Despite his dreadful experiences, he is a generous and loving man, with an ability to provoke emotions in others. There is 'something blessed in his manner' (p. 17): within minutes of his entry into 124 Bluestone Road both Sethe and Denver cry, and Sethe weeps again in the penultimate section of the book (p. 272). At the carnival his good humour is infectious (p. 48). He has learned to focus his affection on inanimate objects: 'loving small and in secret' (p. 221) and he is disturbed by the intensity and power of Sethe's love. He leaves Sethe after Stamp Paid tells him about her action, not because of what she did, but because of the way in which she justifies it. His dream of creating a family unit with her is ruined. He realises that Sethe is much stronger than he had imagined, and that she is not like Halle.

His relationship with Beloved is highly antagonistic. One of his first actions on arrival at the house is to drive the ghost out of it. He resents and questions the presence of the full-grown Beloved, 'a room-and-board witch' (p. 164) and interrogates her about her origins. She moves him out of Sethe's bed and seduces him in the coldroom. His response to the situation is to tell Sethe that he would like to father her child. She gives him a feeling of rootedness. He tells Sethe that when he arrived at her porch he realised (p. 46) that he had been heading towards her and is convinced that they can make a life together. Before, it was sufficient to 'eat, walk and sleep anywhere' (p. 270), but he is moved by Sethe, and wants to live out his life with her (p. 221). The sealed tobacco tin that is a metaphor for his heart breaks open and his suppressed memories fly free. Their pasts are complementary: 'he wants to put his story next to hers' (p. 273) and the possibility of their having a future together necessitates coming to terms with their shared and traumatic past. Like Sethe, Paul D had limited himself to a fulfilment of immediate exigencies and nothing more. When he was roaming America, thinking 'only about the next meal and night's sleep . . . he had no sense of failure, of things not working out. Anything that worked out at all, worked out' (p. 221). Similarly, Sethe believes that her present life with Denver is better precisely because it is not 'that other one' (p. 42). The two of them are forced to confront each other's past and it is this confrontation that gives the novel its force.

Baby Suggs

Although Baby Suggs is dead, she is a prominent character in the novel. She is missed and alluded to by many of the protagonists. Paul D asks after her in the very first section, and Sethe, upon hearing that Halle is dead, longs for the comfort of her massaging fingers. Janey, the servant of the Bodwins, for all her scathing remarks about Sethe and her behaviour, has only 'sweet words' (p. 254) for Baby Suggs. For Denver, the death of her grandmother is one of several losses, and she remembers Baby Suggs telling her stories about her father and promising her that the baby ghost would not hurt her (pp. 207–9). Stamp Paid was originally angry with Baby Suggs's resignation from the world. Later in the novel he comes to understand her final defeatist stance (p. 177):

> sixty years of losing children to the people who chewed up her life . . . five years of freedom given to her by her last child, who bought her future with his . . . to lose him too; to acquire a daughter . . . see that daughter slay the children (or try to); to belong to a community of . . . free Negroes . . . and then have that community step back and hold itself at a distance – well, it could wear out even a Baby Suggs, holy.

Baby Suggs had eight children by six different fathers. Scattered through the narrative are allusions to the pain of never seeing one's children grow. She never saw any of her four daughters in adulthood (p. 139). The people she has known have all 'run off . . . been hanged, got rented out, loaned out, bought up, brought back, stored up, mortgaged, won, stolen or seized'. (p. 23). After Halle has bought her her freedom she tries to reunite her family, but her efforts are thwarted. She focuses all her remaining affection upon Halle and his new family. Baby Suggs's life is a practical example of the brutality of the slave system: the way men and women were moved around like draughts on a board. This is exemplified by the way that her employers misname her for the duration of her working life. She is one of the many women in the narrative who have suffered some degree of sexual abuse. She recounts briefly the way in which she was blackmailed and betrayed by a 'straw boss' who coerced her into 'coupling' with him. He then sold the son that he had fathered (p. 23). Similarly the overseer of the over-full ship, in which her two daughters Nancy and Famous perished, brings her the news of their deaths in the hopes of 'having his way with her' (p. 144) rather than through any altruism.

Her son pays for her freedom. As a slave she has no self, denied of 'the map to discover what she was like' (p. 140). She has been dispossessed of her sense of identity, and, only upon being freed does she regain this sense of identity. In the carriage, she hears her heart beating for the first time. Liberated from oppression, she becomes a formidable and strong woman. While she lives at 124 Bluestone Road it is a focal point for the community: 'a cheerful, buzzing house where Baby Suggs, holy, loved, cautioned, fed, chastised and soothed' (p. 86–7). When Denver begins to meet her neighbours she is regaled with tales of 124 Bluestone Road (p. 249) as it used to be. In Section 9 of Part One of the novel, Sethe describes the services that Baby Suggs held in the Clearing, which earned her the right to be called 'holy'. Her 'great heart' (p. 87) beats in the presence of men, women and children, and she speaks a subversive message of self-love and worthiness. She urges her hearers to love themselves, in contrast to their evaluation by white people: 'And O my people they do not love your hands. They only use, tie, bind, chop off and leave empty' (p. 88). She gave Denver the same message, authorising her right to 'pleasurable feelings' (p. 209) and commanding her to love and respect her body. She was a central figure in the community, but, after Sethe's actions she gave up her role of 'unchurched preacher' and retreated to her bed in order to contemplate colour, regressing to a child-like state. The fact that the system of slavery and the Fugitive Bill permitted Schoolteacher to enter her yard to fetch Sethe – thus precipitating the terrible chain of events – results in Baby Suggs loosing faith in the God she had believed in. Denver paraphrases what her grandmother felt: 'she had done everything right and they came in her yard anyway' (p. 209). The Civil War and the disappearance of her grandsons hardly affect her; instead there is her quiet devotion to colour, which she admires because it does not 'hurt' anything.

For all her strength and wisdom, she is destroyed by Sethe's actions, a fact that Sethe herself acknowledges (p. 183). The last years of her life and her last words show her awareness of the terrible power that white people had over black. The destruction of a woman renowned and loved for her heart, the one thing left intact (p. 87) after a life of slavery, is as tragic as Sethe's reaction to that power. Baby Suggs cannot even be buried in the Clearing due to a rule invented by whites (p. 171) and her funeral is a scene of divisive spite. Before dying she informs Sethe and Denver that:

'there is no bad luck in the world but whitefolks' (p. 89). She holds them responsible for breaking her heart, for stealing all that she owned or for which she dreamed.

Stamp Paid

Stamp Paid has a central role in the events of the novel, both in its present and recounted past. He is the man who meets Sethe and ferries her across the Ohio. He brought the blackberries that started the feast that overstepped the boundaries of propriety. Baby Suggs's extravagent generosity caused the bad feeling that prevented the community from warning the inhabitants of 124 about Schoolteacher's approach. Once more, he is there the next morning, chopping wood as the white men arrive to remove Sethe and the children. He saw Denver shortly after she was born and saved her from being killed by Sethe: he is fond of her. He shows Paul D the newspaper clipping about Sethe, thus precipitating Paul D's departure. It is the thought of Denver, combined with the memory of Baby Suggs that prompts him to try to remedy the damage he has caused through telling Paul D about Sethe.

The tale of Stamp's life, which he recounts to Paul D, demonstrates yet another way in which white people sullied the lives of black people. After his wife, Vashti, was taken from him to please his master's son, Stamp renames himself with his present name. Before, he was called Joshua, which means 'Jehovah-is-salvation'. The act of self-baptism and the choice of his new name, 'Stamp Paid', signifies that he considers himself responsible for his own salvation, that he is debt-free and has no remaining obligations. He devotes the rest of his life to helping others. His payment is always being a welcome visitor, never having to knock on a door. His sense of community is fully developed, as is evidenced by his anger with Ella when he discovers that Paul D has been dossing in the church cellar.

Stamp was a friend of Baby Suggs, and saw her as a woman with the strength of a mountain (p. 181). He realises that he was wrong to upbraid her, and comes to understand her resignation, and why ultimately she renounced her religious duties.

Ella

Together with Stamp Paid, Ella is a woman who helps fugitives to safety. She is the one who meets Sethe at the other side of the Ohio river. Although she had been friends with Baby Suggs, after Sethe's behaviour she does not speak to her, and in eighteen years has only nodded to her at the carnival. She has no patience with Sethe's pride. 'I ain't got no friends take a handsaw to their own children' (p. 187). Despite her strong stance against Sethe, it is Ella who goes to her rescue. She goes to exorcise Beloved, and, when Sethe tries to kill Mr Bodwin, she knocks her out. She is prompted to help Sethe by a fear of 'past errors taking hold of the present' (p. 256). For the same reasons that she disapproves of Sethe's behaviour, she cannot condone Beloved's return and her unrelenting destruction of her mother. Stamp Paid reproaches her for not offering Paul D a bed after he left Sethe's house (p. 186) We learn that she was shared by a white father and his son (p. 256), whom she refers to as 'the lowest yet'. Sethe believes that something similar had happened to Beloved (p. 119). As a consequence, Ella understands Sethe's rage but not her actions. She sees life as a 'test and a trial' (p. 256) and has been beaten 'every way but down' (p. 258).

Lady Jones

Lady Jones runs the school that Denver attended as a child. Denver returns to Lady Jones's house when she realises that she needs to help Sethe. She is of mixed race, and has grey eyes and 'yellow woolly hair' (p. 247). Her light skin meant that she was allowed the benefit of education and she teaches the children of the area for a nickel a month. This is done in the spirit of retaliation: Lady Jones despises herself for not being entirely black, and assumes that this feeling is shared by the rest of the community. She does not share the awe for Baby Suggs that the other characters of the novel express, referring to her in her thoughts as 'the ignorant grandmother'. She is one of the women who scorns the supernatural story of Beloved's return to 124 Bluestone Road.

Mr and Mrs Garner; Schoolteacher

Mr Garner is the proprietor of Sweet Home and the owner of six slaves: Sethe, Halle, Paul D, Paul F, Paul A and Saxo. Garner prides himself on his liberal attitude towards his slaves (pp. 10–11). He believes that his slaves are men in contradistinction to the slaves of his neighbours 'Y'all got boys' (p. 11); Baby Suggs, Sethe's predecessor, recognises the 'special kind of slavery' (p. 140) where Garner treats his slaves as if they were employees. She remembers the smallness of Sweet Home and the fact that 'nobody knocked her down' (p. 139). This phrase is repeated four times which suggests that physical violence was a reality of her former life. She lists the incredible amount of tasks that she completes alongside Mrs Garner – before dismissing it with the phrase: 'nothing to it' (p. 140). Her work on Sweet Home is comparatively easy. Sethe, like Baby Suggs before her, works beside Mrs Garner in the kitchen and in the vegetable garden. The two women, slave and owner, have a relationship of co-operation. Mrs Garner recognises Sethe's desire for some semblance of ceremony when she chooses Halle to be her partner, and gives Sethe a pair of crystal earrings as a present (p. 58). When Sethe is pregnant, a midwife is present. Mrs Garner gives Sethe a piece of cloth to make a dress for her baby (p. 163) and, on her illness, Sethe nurses Mrs Garner as if she was her mother (pp. 193–5). When Sethe tells Mrs Garner about the beating she receives at the hands of Schoolteacher's nephews (p. 202, p. 228) Mrs Garner cannot stop crying.

While the female slaves are not forced to work in the fields and enjoy this relaxed relationship with their mistress, the men were:

> allowed, encouraged to correct Garner, even defy him. To invent ways of doing things; to see what was needed and attack it without permission. To buy a mother, choose a horse or a wife, handle guns, even learn reading if they wanted (p. 125)

Mr Garner allowed Halle to buy his mother's freedom. He accompanies Baby Suggs to Cincinnati and introduces her to the Bodwins. Nevertheless he never questions the name of her bill of sale and calls her Jenny for the duration of her working life. He fully believes that he is responsible for the virility of his male salves, since he is: 'Tough enough and smart enough to make and call his own niggers men.' This reported speech is laden with the rooted attitudes that allowed slavery to exist. Garner, despite the respect with which he treats his slaves, regards them as possessions, 'his own niggers', that he can shape with judicious treatment. While the slaves on Sweet Home appreciate Garner for his generosity, they realise the contradictions inherent in his attitude towards them. The irony is brought out by Halle, who points out that the advantages for Garner in letting him buy Baby Suggs' freedom (pp. 195–6). As the Bodwins make clear, Garner's liberality is nevertheless a 'kind' of slavery (p. 145).

Mr Garner dies unexpectedly of a stroke and the whole structure of Sweet Home and the slaves' lives falls apart. As Paul D bitterly remembers: 'everything rested on Garner being alive . . . Now ain't that slavery, or what is it?' (p. 220). As soon as Mrs Garner is widowed she sells off one of Paul D's brothers. It is imperative that she, a white woman, must not be left alone with her slaves (p. 36). Her husband's brother-in-law, Schoolteacher, arrives, 'to put things in order' (p. 9). He is accompanied by his two nephews (pp. 36–7). He scorns Mr Garner's lax methods (p. 227) and agrees with the neighbours that his brother-in-law had defied normal ways of behaving.

The slaves are no longer allowed to offer their opinions, nor to use guns. Schoolteacher devises a series of 'corrections' to re-educate the slaves, and records everything in his notebook (p. 221). He asks the slaves questions, and Sethe overhears him instructing his nephews to divide her animal and human characteristics (p. 193). Sethe realises that he is researching a 'book about us' (p. 37) and writing it with the ink that she makes. He administers the first of many beatings to take place at Sweet Home (p. 197) and ties Sixo up with the other farm animals for stealing a shoat (p. 223). The slaves are regarded as little more than animals, and Sethe is seen in terms of her biological ability to produce infinite labour for his farm. After Sethe's escape to Cincinnati and the dissolution of Sweet Home, School-teacher appears at 124 Bluestone Road in order to repossess her (p. 148). The sight of him precipitates Sethe's drastic action in the woodshed, just as his attitude convinced her of the necessity of leaving Sweet Home: 'No notebook for my babies, and no measuring string neither' (p. 198). Scholteacher's dehumanising and self-righteous behaviour epitomises one aspect of the evil of slavery.

The Bodwins

Mr and Miss Bodwin, brother and sister, are two Scots who have no sympathy with slavery. They are friends of Mr Garner, and once Baby Suggs's freedom has been bought, he takes her to see them in Cincinnati. They offer her the use of 124 Bluestone Road, and suggest that she mend shoes and take in washing for a living. When Sethe is imprisoned, it is only because of their exertions that she is not hanged for what she has done. Denver is fully aware of their history of having helped her family when she goes to their house in the hope of finding work. They agree to take her on as a night-help and Edward Bodwin drives to 124 to pick her up. He was born there and we hear his nostalgia for his childhood (p. 260) and his reflections on his adult life as an active abolitionist. It is a cruel irony that he should be the one that Sethe attacks in her warped attempt to protect her daughters. As Stamp asserts, it would have been 'the worst thing in the world for us' (p. 265) had Sethe reached him with her ice-pick.

Halle

Halle is the much-loved son of Baby Suggs. He took note of her pain and paid for her freedom with his own labour. He could read and count and was therefore able to calculate the worth of his work. He witnessed Sethe's rape when he was hiding in the barn, and was last seen by Paul D, rubbing butter over his face in the dairy. Baby Suggs claims that she felt him die on the day of Denver's birth (p. 8). Denver craves the father she has never known, listening avidly to her grandmother's anecdotes about him (p. 208) and envisaging a fantasy scenario in which he comes back to live with her and Beloved. The absence of information as to Halle's fate is a significant gap in the texture of Toni Morrison's narrative: 'Nobody knows what happened' (p. 224). This testifies to her commitment to illustrating a ver-sion of history that is very different from the cut-and-dried facts of history books, showing the messiness of real life as opposed to the neatly aligned columns in Schoolteacher's notebooks.

Sixo

Sixo figures prominently in Paul D's memories of Sweet Home. He was the only one of the Sweet Home men who did not desire Sethe. Instead he planned to marry a woman who lived thirty miles away and Paul D relates his meetings with her (pp. 24, 222). Sixo represents the manhood that Paul D feels he is lacking, and it is significant that he imagines Sixo as his judge when he leaves Sethe (p. 267). Sixo is close to his tribal roots: he stops speaking English because he sees it as a language without a future and dances at night to keep his bloodlines open (p. 25). When he sings it is another language, but 'hatred so loose it was juba' (p. 227). In the thwarted escape from Sweet Home, Sixo resists capture and is tied to a tree. Schoolteacher and the other men are unable to set him on fire, and have to shoot him to stop him singing (pp. 225–6). This act of violence is ostensibly recounted by Paul D. Its horror is not diminished by the use of narrative tricks but is told in a stark and chilling present tense.

Amy Denver

Amy is the white girl who helps with Denver's birth and Sethe's survival. Significantly her name means friend or beloved. Strong-armed and shock-headed, she too is in search of softness in the North. She is the probable offspring of an indentured servant and her master. At eighteen she is a year younger than Sethe. She is yet to have children, while Sethe is pregnant with her fourth child. Although she is 'the raggediest looking trash you ever saw' (pp. 31–2) she travels at liberty while Sethe fears recapture and further violations.

Amy renames the marks on Sethe's back as a tree, transforming her scars from their association of death and pain to a thing of growth and beauty. Her chatter silences the baby and she wraps Sethe's feet. Together they form a temporary family unit of sorts in the absence of society's values, represented by the reference to 'no patroller' and 'no preacher' (p. 85). Amy leaves her mark in Denver's name. She is a primary instance of Toni Morrison's reluctance to vilify white people or valorise blacks, although by the end of the novel Sethe and Baby Suggs have no patience for any white people at all.

Structure

The novel is split into three parts of unequal length. The first part is subdivided into eighteen sections, the second into seven, and the third into two and an epilogue. All three of the main parts open with a similar phrase. This repetition cannot but be noticed by the reader and draws attention to a progression in the state of events portrayed in the novel.

In the beginning, Sethe's home is rocked by Beloved's activities, limited at this point to poltergeist manifestations: '124 was spiteful' (p. 3). In Part One we witness the arrival and departure of Paul D, Beloved's appearance in flesh and blood, and the awful events in the woodshed, related through the perceptions of a variety of protagonists. Although the narrative proceeds over the course of a year, the body of the text relates the events of the past. Part Two starts with the phrase: '124 was loud' (p. 169). The house is roaring with the voices of the oppressed, the 'people of the broken necks, of fire-cooked blood, and black girls who had lost their ribbons' (p. 181). This part contains the interior monologues by Beloved, Sethe and Denver, and the latter two's acceptance of Beloved's identity as daughter and sister. It ends with Paul D's impassioned questioning of Stamp Paid as to how much suffering he, as a black man, is expected to withstand.

In Part Three '124 was quiet' (pp. 239, 242). This part chronicles Denver's release into the world outside 124 Bluestone Road, while her mother and sister continue their battle of love and guilt. The lack of food and exhaustion subdues Beloved, and the house is quiet. Beloved disappears and Sethe takes to her bed. It closes with the possibility of a future life as Paul D returns to the house and pledges his commitment to a 'tomorrow' with Sethe.

The shortness of the sentence, containing the most basic arrangement of noun, verb and adjective, signals a significance in the break-up of the narrative. This conscious structuring imposes an order on the meandering narrative, the mixture of tenses, periods of time and first-person voices that compose *Beloved*. The three key phrases underline the progression of events, and emphasise the location and development of these events in the immediate present of the novel as the house evolves through various stages, acting as a symbol for a similar evolution in the lives of its inhabitants.

Language

In 1993 Toni Morrison was awarded the Nobel Prize for Literature. In her address she relates a story of an elderly blind woman, famed for her wisdom, which some children attempt to challenge, by presenting her with a bird. They ask her whether it is alive or dead. She answers by telling them that it is in their hands. Toni Morrison goes on to interpret this story as an analogy of a writer and the language she uses. What she says illustrates how fully she appreciates the power inherent in language both as a medium and an instrument. She acknowledges its complex properties and its capacity as a tool for and agent of oppression, but concludes by suggesting that the human capacity to 'do language' and to make meaning may be 'the measure of our lives'. Similarly in the preface to her critical work, *Playing in the Dark: Whiteness and the Literary Imagination* she comments on her awareness that 'language can powerfully evoke and enforce hidden signs of racial superiority, cultural hegemony, and dismissive "othering" of people and language'.

Beloved is testimony to Toni Morrison's stated appreciation and her ability to manipulate language. She makes use of varying lexical implications of words in her narrative. When Paul D looks at Sethe, 'the word "bad" took on another meaning' (p. 7). Words can have different meanings, or to use the phraseology of the philologist Saussure, signs can have different signifiers. Sethe uses the word 'nurse' to describe the way she was forced to suckle two grown men. The associations of breast-feeding and babies, and consequentially of protection and love, conjured up by the verb 'nurse', bring home the horror of the situation to the reader. This inappropriacy is also present in the incongruous name of the farm to which Denver draws attention (p. 13), for Sweet Home was neither 'sweet' nor 'home' for the slaves who lived there. Similarly Toni Morrison plays with the misnaming of the location of her earlier novel, *Sula* (1974). The black community live in an area called Bottom, oddly enough situated at the top of the valley.

The bodies of the protagonists convey a language of their own. Sethe is a marked woman in the same way that her mother and Beloved are, all bearing scars that 'write' their slavery. The novel explores the way in which the bodies of black women, as the site for reproduction, reveal stories of the past that were ignored in male slave-narratives. Paul D prevents Sethe from 'reading' the signs that mark Beloved as her daughter: the scar under her chin and the thin scratches on her forehead.

While Denver makes her link to the black community through writing (she goes to Lady Jones's house, where she first learnt to read, and uses this skill to decipher the notes that are left with the food that her neighbours give her), non-written modes of communication bolster the narrative: the songs that Paul D sings as he mends the furniture, or works in the chain-gang, Amy's mother's song, or the song that Sethe has made up to sing to her children, and which Beloved is found singing. Most importantly, Toni Morrison deliberately mines the rich tradition of story-telling, that is, and was, so much a feature of black culture long before print existed.

The substance of the novel, mediated largely via the thoughts and spoken words of its protagonists, rarely takes the form of structured sentences. Instead, the narrative is peppered with rhetorical questions, semi-repetitions and half-sentences: it also jumps without warning from present to past and far past, all of which lend verisimilitude and vitality to the novel.

As in music, where pauses and silence have an essential role, so in this novel silence speaks volumes: 'Ella . . . listened for the holes – the things fugitives did not say; the questions they did not ask. Listened too for the unnamed, unmentioned people left behind' (p. 92).

All her techniques draw attention to language's living properties, but there also exists a negative and deadening aspect of its power. Words are the cause of Denver's deafness: in order not to hear the answer that she dreads, she closes herself off from all sound. The illegible 'black scratches' (p. 155) of the newspaper that Stamp shows Paul D contain words that are powerless to *explain* Sethe's act (p. 161). Sixo stops speaking English because he sees no future in it (p. 25), illustrating the danger for the first Afro-Americans, condemned to creating their identity via a language that was not their own. Since slaves on their arrival in America came from a variety of ethnic groups and spoke different African languages they were forced to adopt English to communicate. In her speech when she received the Nobel Prize, Toni Morrison dwells on the susceptibility of language to death and erasure. Dead language is a danger that a writer must identify, and use techniques to avoid. *Beloved* is replete with these techniques.

Style

Toni Morrison uses the present tense throughout *Beloved*, although the narrative spans a period of some fifty years, stretching back to Baby Suggs's youth and Sethe's earliest memories of her mother. The prevalence and priority given to memories and remembering obscure the boundaries of time so often used to structure literary works. Morrison flouts the confines of physical presence and consciousness by which novelists are usually restricted. While in her earlier novels she made use of premonitions, visions and coincidences, in *Beloved*, she unambiguously endorses the supernatural. One of the characters is a ghost. The novel, like the miserable house as 124 Bluestone Road, pulsates with unnatural energy.

Moreover the readers are denied vital knowledge: we neither learn why Beloved has appeared, nor where she has gone. The shifting voice of the narrator, which flits in and out of different characters' thoughts, conveys a similar process of defamiliarisation for the reader. We hear the cogitation's of Edward Bodwin (pp. 259–61), the thought processes of School-teacher (pp. 149–51), and Stamp Paid's voice, as well as that of the central protagonists.

In Part Two of the novel there are four sections that represent the interior monologues of Sethe, Denver and Beloved. Those that belong to Beloved are most interesting when we come to consider the novel's style.

The first of these is completely unpunctuated. Its language and content are highly repetitive and circular. It represents a time and place beyond the constructs of sentences and sense: the place from which Beloved came and where she existed as a spirit. It is possible to read this in terms of theories, appropriated by feminist critics, that children, before they succumb to the patriarchal dictates of formalised language, perceive the world through a female language that has an entirely different set of rules, shunning a linear time-scale, 'all of it is now' (p. 210) in favour of patterning. (For those interested, this can be traced via Freud, Lacan and Kristeva.) This supports our sense of Beloved being a baby. The technique of stream of consciousness is by no means invented by Toni Morrison. It was first used by a French writer, Valérie Larbaud (1881–1951) and elaborated in the profuse and multiple thoughts of Bloom in James Joyce's (1882–1941) *Ulysses* (1922) and Virginia Woolf's (1882–1941) writings. Here the style is accentuated, even on a typographical level, so we cannot but be aware that Morrison is disregarding the common rules of writing. Nevertheless, this style is not confined to Beloved's thoughts alone, but is used, to some extent, throughout the novel. This means that there is no fixed point of reference for the reader, as memories meld and flow. Sethe's violent act in the woodshed is related from several different viewpoints: Baby Suggs, Stamp, Schoolteacher and Sethe herself. The reader is given no indication of whether they are expected to approve or otherwise. We are forced to relive the same scene many times, and the facts of the baby's death are present from the very first pages of the novel.

These techniques and others mean that *Beloved* is open-ended. Morrison aspires to this quality and identifies incompletion as a feature of black music:

> Jazz always keeps you on the edge. There is no final chord . . . Spirituals agitate you . . . There is something underneath them that is incomplete . . . I want my books to be like that . . . I want that feeling of something held in reserve and the sense that there is more . . .
>
> (N. McKay, 'An Interview with Toni Morrison')

Music is a rich source of metaphor for Morrison and is referred to in the preface of *Playing in the Dark*, as well as being used as a structural and thematic principle in her novel, *Jazz*. She aims to unsettle her readers by drawing their attention to the gaps in her narrative. Morrison states explicitly: 'I must use my craft to make the reader see the colours and hear the sounds' (see C. Tate, 'A Conversation with Toni Morrison'). Sound is central to her style of prose poetry. For example, the phrase: 'Sifting daylight dissolves the memory, turns it into dust motes floating in light' (p. 264) with its assonance of sibilants or 's' sounds in 'sifting . . . dissolves' and the hinted rhyme of 'motes . . . float(ing)' reveals a studied arrangement of words to create effect.

Toni Morrison plays with repetition, a musical device, repeating memories and images within the novel, and, on a more local level, uses repetition as a device to recreate the thought processes of her characters. An example of this is in Section 1 of the first part of the novel, where we hear Denver's reiteration of Paul D's words: 'only those who knew him well ("knew him well")' and her own weariness 'wear her out. Wear her out' (p. 13). The same phrase is later repeated in the past tense (p. 29). In Section 2 sexual tension is built up by a highly eroticised account of the preparation of corn. The voyeurism in which Paul D and the other men engage while watching the corn move as Halle and Sethe have sex is reflected by a lingering and repetitive description of the way in which they prepare the damaged corn to eat that evening (p. 27). Sethe and Paul D's memories blend and fuse together. The phrase 'How loose the silk' is repeated four times with only one variation. The choral effect slows down the narrative, and recreates a sense of satiety in the reader. Repetition of a phrase is similarly used to create a sense of calm, as it imitates the rising and falling of Paul D's chest as he sleeps (p. 132). The device is also employed to imbue a sense of panic into the narrative. Paul D tells Stamp that the picture of Sethe is not her, since her mouth is drawn incorrectly. The phrase: 'That ain't her mouth' is repeated seven times (pp. 154–9) and does much to embody Paul D's stubborn refusal to accept Stamp's tale. When Sethe and the two girls go skating the phrase 'Nobody saw them falling' is repeated many times (p. 174) and effectively establishes the unity of the three women. This is one point in which the reader is made aware of their position as audience and outsider.

Imagery

Animal–Human

Beloved chronicles a period of radical change and redefinition for emancipated black people. As slaves they had been dependent on whites for their entire existence; they now found themselves without the material or emotional means to cope with freedom. Paul D describes with horror the black women, men and children that he saw before, during and after the Civil War (p. 66). He himself stole from pigs and 'fought owls' for food, whilst being hunted like a beast. He recalls a 'witless colored woman' who was under the delusion that ducks were her children, identifying with the birds themselves. This confusion of boundaries is also present at Sweet Home, where, in the absence of women, the men were 'fucking cows' and had 'taken to calves' (pp. 10–11). It is perhaps this alignment of cows with women which imbues Paul D's reproach to Sethe with power. When she tells him of her attempted killing of her children, he responds by informing her that she has two legs, and not four.

Throughout the novel Toni Morrison makes telling use of vocabulary to highlight the boundaries and differences between animal and human. Sethe feels the indignity of being treated as a goat by Schoolteacher's nephews, her swollen breasts milked by two grown men. The milk destined for her children is appropriated and she is reduced to the status of an animal. Schoolteacher describes his slaves as if they were animals, albeit animals in his care. He regards Sethe as a creature that God has given him the responsibility of maintaining (p. 149). These common attitudes legitimised the de-humanising way in which white owners treated their slaves. That Schoolteacher is convinced that black people are scarcely distinguishable from beasts is evinced by his research measurements and the conversation that Sethe overhears in which he requests his nephews to align her animal and human characteristics (p. 193). When Schoolteacher witnesses what Sethe has done to her children in the woodshed he attributes her behaviour to the excessive beating she received at the hands of his nephews. He makes an analogy with what would have happened had his nephews similarly beaten a horse or dog (p. 149).

The language of domestic animals, particularly horses, is often used by white people when describing their slaves. The planned escape from Sweet Home is described as a 'stampede' (p. 226), a noun associated with the wild movement of animals. Sethe's youngest baby is referred to by the neutral noun 'foal' (p. 227) while Amy asks Sethe if she is just going to 'foal' (p. 33), using the same word as a verb. Amy's casual acceptance of racial constructions and difference emphasises the racial hierarchy that persists even between two 'throw-away' people (pp. 84–5) such as herself and Sethe. Despite their moment of unity by the riverside, Amy's whiteness places her above Sethe.

The dehumanisation of black slaves was embodied in the white attitude to their having children, the inevitable fruits of sex. Men and women were used to 'stud', and regarded as nothing more than a species of farm animal. Sethe is regarded as a valuable possession since she is 'property that reproduced itself without cost' (p. 228). As a woman she is capable of 'breeding' (pp. 149, 227) and furnishing the farm with new free labour. The more brutal aspects of slavery are hidden from the slaves while Mr Garner lives. Sethe is allowed the delusion of a wedding and honeymoon. Nevertheless, the importance of her capacity to produce is implicit in Mrs Garner's question when she learns that Sethe is getting married: 'Are you already expecting?' (p. 26). This attitude meant that black people were prevented from enjoying sex or loving their children, as Baby Suggs tells Denver:

> Slaves not supposed to have pleasurable feelings ... but they have to have as many children as they can to please whoever owned them (p. 209).

The attitudes that permitted the studding of humans are consonant with those that allowed the destruction of family bonds and the selling of other human beings. Toni Morrison emphasises the utter depravity of slavery by emphasising the concepts of humanity and bestiality.

Water

The image of water runs through *Beloved*. The Ohio River is the boundary that Sethe identifies between herself and freedom. She has no wish to die 'on the bloody side of the Ohio River' (p. 31). Once she has crossed the river she is free and can begin a new life. On seeing the river her waters break 'to join it' (p. 83) and she gives birth to Denver. She drinks water from the river, determined not to die on the 'wrong side' (p. 90). When she arrives at 124 Bluestone Road Baby Suggs washes her in sections; purifying her after the ravages of her old life. In the last part of the book, Paul D offers to wash Sethe (p. 272). It is a deeply symbolic gesture, and Toni Morrison emphasises this for the reader, as Sethe wonders whether he will repeat Baby Suggs's gestures, thus alluding to the possibility of a new life.

Beloved emerges from the water (p. 50), reborn as an adult. On arrival at 124 Bluestone Road she drinks four cupfuls of water. Sethe remembers her baby's dribbling 'clear spit' on her face (p. 93) and, in retrospect, connects this with the water that Beloved drank (p. 202). When Sethe first sees Beloved her bladder overflows and she experiences an artificial delivery. She herself acknowledges the similarity to her waters breaking at Denver's birth (p. 51). Toni Morrison makes a series of references to rivers, rain, snow and ice throughout the novel. They are all positive.

References to water are paralleled by Toni Morrison's recurring use of two other liquids: milk and blood, both tarnished with negative associations. Sethe's milk is stolen from her. The clabber on Halle's face by the butter churn is symbolic of the way in which their family structure has been soured and ruined by slavery. Beloved's blood soaks the narrative, and her death, occurring after twenty-eight days of freedom, 'the travels of one whole moon' (p. 95) alludes to the flow of the menstrual cycle. Water, on the other hand is *aqua vitae*, it symbolises cleanliness and rebirth.

Food

Sethe uses the metaphor of hunger to describe her brain's willingness to accept the horrors of the past. She characterises her mind as a greedy child who will not refuse food. Beloved is the greedy child of the novel, devouring sugar and, finally, Sethe herself. She can be appeased by hearing tales of Sethe's past: 'It became a way to feed her' (p. 58) and sweet things or news can be relied upon to give her pleasure (p. 74). Denver's relationship with Beloved is also characterised with food imagery. Denver's loneliness before her advent is a hunger, and being looked at by Beloved is 'food enough to last'. Excess of food caused the disapproval amongst the black neighbours that prevented them warning Sethe of the advance of School-teacher and the slave-catcher. Sethe's food was spurned at Baby Suggs's funeral. It is the necessity of food that forces Denver out of Bluestone Road and into the world, and it is by gifts of food that Denver is integrated into community life.

Themes

Treatment of Time

The time-scale of *Beloved* is anything but linear. The narrative progresses in leaps and bounds, and stories are begun and left off, to be resumed again over the course of chapters. An example of this is the story of Denver's birth. It is begun by Denver in Section 3 of Part One of the novel. It is then resumed in Section 8, told by Denver, but experienced through the persona of Sethe. The breaking of Sethe's waters has, however, already been alluded to earlier (p. 51), and Amy's description of the tree on her back is present in Section 1 of this part (p. 16). Halfway through Section 9 the story continues, cataloguing Sethe's arrival at 124 Bluestone Road, and Baby Suggs's patient setting to rights of the damage done by the journey and the white boys. The same technique is used with the details of Sweet Home, Sethe and Halle's marriage, Stamp Paid's life or Paul D's experiences. The escape from Sweet Home is slowly pieced together. Toni Morrison's choice of narrative technique is very condensed. The metaphors are self-reflexive, referring to a context and experiences already established by the novel. When describing the pleasure Denver derives from being scrutinised by Beloved, the metaphor is consonant with Denver's own experience, and makes no reference to the outside world. Her skin grows soft and bright like 'the lisle dress that had her arms round her mother's waist' (p. 118). The reader recognises this reference to the vision that appeared to Denver (p. 29), and a series of links are forged within the novel's imagery. Similarly, characters refer to events that are explained much later to the reader. Paul D in Section 1, talking to Sethe about Halle, resolves that she need never know about her husband's dereliction by the butter churn (p. 8). The reference to the appalling scene of Halle by the churn makes no sense to the reader, but is later unpacked and given resonance (p. 69). Similarly the reference to Sixo's last laugh (p. 41) is later padded out (p. 229). This technique creates an intensity that cannot but be felt by the reader.

In many respects, part of the novel's interest, horror and beauty lies in the way in which Sethe and Paul D come to terms with their memories, allowing the reader to share the pain of their lives. Paul D says to Sethe that together they have 'more yesterday than anybody. We need some kind of tomorrow' (p. 273). Sethe has already acknowledged this factor: 'Her story was bearable because it was his as well – to tell, to refine, and to tell again' (p. 99). She also comments on the impossibility of making plans:

> her brain was not interested in the future. Loaded with the past and hungry for more, it left her no room to imagine, let alone plan for, the next day (p. 70).

Beloved charts the exorcism of this 'yesterday' in order to facilitate a future for its protagonists. The character of Beloved is an embodiment of the past, and her appearance stimulates Denver's maturity. She is forgotten and the novel comes to a close. Significantly, when Sethe fully realises that Beloved is her daughter, she goes to work wrapped in a 'timeless present' (p. 184). She abandons her adult responsibilities towards the future. She loses her job, spends her life-savings on clothes, and defies temporality by planting a garden out of season. Sethe feels that she can jettison the burden of her past since Beloved is back. Unfortunately her guilt is not so easily absolved, as she is punished by her daughter and by herself. Only at the close of the novel are we left with a feeling that Sethe's turbulent past has been put to rest. Up to this point, which only occurs in the epilogue, the past has had a central role in the novel. It is characterised as a force, leaping in and out of the narrative: 'to Sethe, the future was a matter of keeping the past at bay' (p. 42), something that has to be suppressed with aggression, 'the day's work of beating back the past' (p. 73). The power of the past is demonstrated by the near constant use of the present tense. Remembered experience is sufficiently vivid to overpower the boundaries of time. It is only in the epilogue that Toni Morrison employs a definitive past tense and the distancing that this entails.

The significance of memory emphasises the power of the past in the novel. Sethe explains her theories to Denver (p. 36), telling her that nothing ever dies, and that the pictures and images of things remain, independent of the existence and experiences of their protagonists. Sethe refers to her 'rememory' and later uses the word 'disremember' to describe self-willed forgetting (p. 118). These unexpected prefixes startle the reader into an awareness of the importance of remembered events. After all, they form the body of the novel. We are sensitised to the process of buried and suppressed memories and, along with the protagonists, we are involved in the process of excavation.

Naming

Names have significance in *Beloved*. The choosing of a name is an assertion of self-love and freedom, while the imposition of a name often implies a relationship of dominance and power. These themes have obvious links with the issues of slavery and oppression that form the historical context for the novel.

White people have the power to define the slaves who work for them. Sixo attempts to use Schoolteacher's own rationalisation to justify his theft of a young pig and is beaten to remind him that 'definitions belonged to the definers – not the defined' (p. 190). Paul D wonders whether he is a man or whether his manhood is something that Mr Garner has conferred on him. We learn that Garner prided himself on having men and not boys on his farm (pp. 10–11): 'Bought em thataway, raised em thataway', and regards himself as someone who is: 'tough enough and smart enough to make and call his own niggers men'. Here, in 'make and call', the processes of creation and naming are paralleled. A name announces an identity. When Paul D, wearing the bit, with his half-brothers gone and his plans for escape awry, sees a rooster strutting at liberty, he is struck by their relative positions. The rooster, ironically enough, is called 'Mister', an appellation that Paul D, as a slave, is unlikely to hear. Moreover, 'even if you cooked him, you'd still be cooking a rooster named Mister' (p. 72). Thanks to the actions of Schoolteacher, Paul D feels that he has lost his own identity and he is even unsure of his manhood. The fact that School-teacher denies his slaves the use of guns represents a symbolic emascula-tion: the guns can be read as phallic symbols. Schoolteacher and Garner share the same basic attitude; that the men who work for them are posses-sions, unformed substances that, with the right treatment, can be 'made' into men, or well-behaved beasts. Being a man and subsequent manliness is not inherent, but conferred. This linguistic relationship between giver and received, the namer and the named, reflects the power-relationship between the white owner and his black slaves. It is illustrated by the unimaginative and dehumanising names that Mr Garner gives the three half-brothers: Paul A, Paul D and Paul F. They are distinguished by a letter and no more. After he has left Sethe and is sitting on the church steps, Paul D contemplates this issue (p. 220):

> Garner called and announced them men – but only on Sweet Home, and by his leave. Was he naming what he saw, or creating what he did not? . . . Did a whiteman saying it make it so?

He wonders what would have happened if Garner had taken the word away. Would he cease to be a man? The shifting nature of words and language, and Paul D's insecurity have already been established in the first part of the book. Paul D lies next to Sethe and looks at her scarred back. He remembers his fondness for a tree he called 'Brother'. Here Paul D is exercising his own power of possession. By giving a tree a name he is making it his, in the same way that Sethe tried to personalise Mrs Garner's kitchen by decorating it with sprigs of herbs. He also recalls Sixo and his sixty-mile trip to see his woman. Paul D reflects: 'Now there was a man, and that was a "tree". Himself lying in the bed and the tree next to him, didn't compare' (p. 22). Words can have many levels of meaning and points of reference. The 'tree' on Sethe's back is not a tree although it is called so. Is Paul D not a man, although he has that name? Similarly Baby Suggs emphasises the importance of naming in relationships: 'A man ain't nothing but a man . . . But a son? Well, now that's *somebody*' (p. 23).

The Garners call Baby Suggs by the name of her bill-of-sale, Jenny Whitlow, the surname being that of her former owner, in the same way a child takes its father's surname. This draws attention to the distorted paternal ethic that characterised slavery. Inhuman treatment was justified in the minds of white people because they saw their slaves as children or animals that needed guidance and could be trained and subdued.

Names can also be chosen. Stamp Pain rechristens himself as an assertion of power. He rejects the name of Joshua, after having given up his wife to his master's son. From then on he feels no obligation to anybody and devotes his life to helping others. Sethe's mother gives her the name of the only man she ever accepted, the only man she ever put her arms around. By doing so she commemorates her right to choose children and husband, in the same way as she exercises that right by throwing away the nameless children of the crew-members who violated her. Baby Suggs opts for the surname of the one man she regards as a husband, although six have fathered her children. She keeps the pet-name that he called her for a first name. Sethe calls her daughter after the strong-armed white girl who helped her. In naming her baby after Amy, Sethe acknowledges the white girl as kin responsible for Denver's birth. Although Amy resumes her quest for velvet, she insists that the baby be cognisant of her role. Denver, when she first meets Paul D, is reproved by her mother for calling him 'Mr D' (p. 11). When she meets him in the last section of the book, she calls him Mr D once again (p. 266), exercising her independence and new maturity.

The issue of naming illustrates Morrison's fundamental worries about language. Names can be appropriated and used to impose ideologies and identities, just as language can be manipulated according to the codes of the user and the reader.

The figure of the mother

Woman's maternal role is central to the text. 'Mammy' is a popular stereotype in European and American film. Fat and nurturing, she is a white distortion of the African view that all mothers are symbols of the marvellous creativity of the earth. Paradoxically, black slave women were, in fact, rarely able to fulfil this stereotype, actively prevented by the exigencies of slave life. This is historically attested by Sojourner Truth's famous 'Ain't I a woman' speech (1852) in which she asserted the experience of black motherhood as a loss:

> I have borne thirteen children and seen most all sold into slavery and when I cried out a mother's grief, none but Jesus heard me.
>
> (C. Boyce Davis, *Black Women Writing and Identity*)

Sethe was suckled by another woman (p. 203), slept apart from her mother, and recognised her by the hat she wore while working and the mark she bore on her ribs (p. 61). Although Sethe's mother claimed her daughter by naming her, in the penultimate section of the novel, we hear Sethe's feelings of pain and resentment enunciated, as Sethe tells Paul D that 'her ma'am' had hurt her feelings (p. 272). She is determined to get her milk to her baby daughter because she has experienced the sensation of being denied the sustenance that was her right.

Baby Suggs is prevented by the system of slavery and persecution from living out her life as a mother. She is denied the possibility of knowing her children as adults, and, by the time of Halle's birth, has given up hope (p. 23) of ever being able to keep her children near her. She accepts the fact that her children are destined to be pawns in a game of checkers instigated, controlled and played by white people. Sethe rebels against these societal values of the time, that inhibited the black mother's capacity to love, and indulges in a 'thick' love, evinced as much by her defence of Denver from Paul D's criticism (p. 45) – and recognised by him as such – as by her violent act in the woodshed. The value vested in a female slave's capacity to reproduce was often manipulated as a form of resistance and there are many records of feigned illness, deliberate miscarriages and self-imposed sterility.

In *Beloved*, milk and breasts are used as a signifier for motherhood. Many black women were forced to suckle the children of white women. The way Sethe's rights as a black mother are impinged upon is symbolised by the way in which she is robbed of her milk. When Sethe is half-strangled in the Clearing, the realisation that Beloved's breath smells of new milk (p. 98) identifies her as Sethe's daughter. Sethe's behaviour in killing her baby daughter can be read as an attempt to reclaim her maternal rights and function. It is an act of protection, of putting her babies into safety, which paradoxically becomes an act of extermination. Several slave mothers committed Sethe's fictional crime, and the text focuses on this historical fact. Toni Morrison herself admits the compulsion: 'to deal with this nurturing instinct that expressed itself as murder' (quoted by C. Boyce Davis). Already in *Sula*, her second novel, Toni Morrison examined the mother's right to kill. Eva sets fire to her son with the intent of 'saving' him. Sethe regards her children as possessions that she has made, and Toni Morrison questions whether this is an appropriate stance for a mother to take.

There is an essential conflict between mothering and being an individual. When Sethe first arrives at 124 Bluestone Road Baby Suggs refers to her as 'the mother' (p. 92). She is defined by her biological role. Sethe allows her children to take precedence over herself. She claims that they are the most important things in her life, and shocks Baby Suggs by telling her that she would not take a breath without them. Sethe would die to protect her Denver (p. 99) and tells the unrelenting Beloved that she would renounce her life in its entirety in order to erase just one of Beloved's tears (p. 242). Sethe's mother love is stifling, and Denver must leave the house before she can become a person in her own right, the confident adult whom Paul D encounters, providing for her mother and keeping her room and her life in order. Exclusive mother love of this nature is not endorsed by the text, and as a motive for Sethe killing her daughter, is neither condoned nor condemned – the style and structure of the text resists a single interpretation. The presence of Paul D liberates Sethe as a character, allowing us to learn of her existence before she was over-determined by her role as mother. However the arrival of Beloved as a living embodiment of Sethe's mother love and of the painful past of enslavement refocuses the conflict between Sethe's individuality and the overpowering love of motherhood.

Nevertheless, the final expulsion of Beloved and the return of Paul D promise a new future and re-integration into the community from which Sethe has been exiled. Her last words 'Me? Me?' (p. 273) in response to Paul D's suggestion that she herself is her own best thing, suggest the possibility of an identity other than the self-imposed role of mother.

Community and Family

Toni Morrison has admitted (to Robert Stepto) her 'tendency . . . to focus on neighbourhoods and families'. In her three earliest works, women, and in particular trios of women attempt to hold whole families together: for example, Pilate in *Song of Solomon* (1977), together with her daughter Reba and granddaughter Hagar, or Eva the one-legged matriarch in *Sula* (1974). In both these novels, the fathers, like Halle in *Beloved*, are absent. Black families historically adapted and changed in reaction to social, political and economic notions of an oppressive society, and during the period of slavery and the years following it, this was especially so.

In *Beloved* Toni Morrison presents a ghastly reworking of the successful trio of women of her former works. The grandmother, Baby Suggs, is dead, and the threesome is composed of a homicidal mother, a matricidal ghostly daughter and the resentful Denver, a trio as ominous as the shadows holding hands that Sethe sees. The family is utterly dysfunctional, deprived of males, and characterised by role-swapping between Sethe and her daughters. Toni Morrison is constantly playing with variants of the nuclear structure and in *Beloved* shows its impossibility, while alluding to the existence of something much larger and more powerful.

In *Beloved* every character is significant, and the reader may be impressed as much by pivotal characters as by the blood relations from which they derive a sense of themselves, such as Baby Suggs, dead during the course of the novel, but so vitally portrayed. In *Beloved* all characters contribute to the whole. The thumbnail sketch of Lady Jones (p. 247) is as relevant as the squalid details of Stamp Paid and his wife, or Ella and the 'lowest yet' (p. 256). This refusal to privilege pays homage to the African concept of neighbourhood; kinship and responsibilities override a narrow family structure.

It is exactly this system of family life that slavery denied black people. Until he meets Sethe, Paul D is resigned to a life without 'aunts, cousins, children' (p. 221). He recounts the impression that large families make on him (p. 219). The semblance of a community that he was allowed to experience at Sweet Home is easily destroyed once Schoolteacher arrives. After her escape Sethe enjoyed only twenty-eight days of community living, experiencing freed life and 'days of healing, ease and real-talk' (pp. 95, 173). It is this concept of shared responsibility that informs Stamp Paid's altruism, as he helps runaways cross the river, and brings messages and food. His anger is great when he discovers that Paul D has been sleeping at the church (p. 186). The power of the community to nurture and sustain its members can also destroy. For Baby Suggs, being abandoned by her community (p. 177), the lack of compassion and understanding from those whom she has known and helped, contributes to her exhaustion, her renunciation of responsibility, and finally her death.

Paul D takes Sethe and Denver out of their isolation and into society when he persuades them to accompany him to the carnival. The three are united with each other and with the community: 'No longer the freaks themselves, they set aside the acutely painful otherness of their condition and blend into the diverse and chaotic circus of humanity', comments one critic, D. Heinze. However, this is only a momentary acceptance. Full reintegration is promised from the point at which Denver resolves to seek help for her mother and makes her difficult re-entry into the world outside 124: she is instrumental in healing the rift between her mother and the black community. She begins to find gifts of food, and, on going to thank the first of her benefactors, hears the single and significant word, 'welcome' (p. 249). It is the community of women, led by Ella, that takes it upon themselves to save Sethe, the action one of familial love and concern. Sethe, like Sula, has been a useful scapegoat for the community, but Beloved, the living threat from the past, is recognised by Ella (p. 256) and must be exorcised. *Beloved* commemorates the resources that allowed slaves, in spite of dehumanising conditions, to love themselves and each other.

Part 4

Hints for study

Toni Morrison's stature as one of the foremost Afro-American female writers of the twentieth century has provoked detailed study from both critics and academics. There are many books and articles which interpret her works according to various theories. A selection of these is listed at the end of this book. However, although it is interesting to see the different ways in which she is interpreted – and knowledge of secondary works will improve your exam answers – nevertheless, very little is more important than familiarising yourself with the text. If you have read and reread *Beloved* you will be able to answer any question, illustrating your response with references to the text. You will be able to provide exceptions and illustrations for other people's critical theories that will personalise your own response. Reading Toni Morrison's other works will allow you to place *Beloved* in context. They are set in different time periods but are all concerned with the injustice and difficulties of the black condition. Various themes – for example, her portrayal of community, family and women – are developed throughout her work.

When reading, it is useful to get into the habit of making notes. Be sure to write the page number so that you can find your references quickly. It is helpful to group themes or recurring images together; for example, in *Beloved* there are many metaphors which refer to food and its function as a gift to be accepted or refused (see p. 57). Think about Baby Suggs's obsession with colour, and the flashes of colour that appear in the narrative like the patches in her quilt: the red ribbon that Stamp finds on the riverbed, the cardinal's red crest, the pink gravestone, or Mister's red comb. This could be tied in with the social implications of the differences between black and white, or with the sparing way in which Morrison describes physical objects. Another recurring image is that of containers and containment. Remember that writing is a totally conscious activity. Morrison does not make use of vocabulary or repetition in a random fashion, but in order to achieve a calculated effect. For this reason do not limit your reading to an understanding of the plot, but think about the language that she uses or the way in which the plot is unravelled.

In an examination situation it is impressive if you are able to quote phrases from the text. Once you have formulated your ideas about Morrison, choose a few quotations that illustrate your theories and memorise them. They should be apposite and word-perfect. There is no need to attempt to commit to memory large chunks of the text: often a few words will suffice to demonstrate your familiarity with the novel. For example, if you are writing about Sethe as a character, or as an example of Morrison's attitude to women or mothers, you could refer to the way in which she defines safety 'with a handsaw' (p. 164).

Practise writing essays in situations as similar as possible to those of an exam. Examination papers are set with a lot of thought behind them, so there is always plenty to say. Read your choice of questions carefully and do not be tempted to pour out all that you know about a novel. An examiner looks for the ways in which students make use of their material, and the manner in which they respond to the question. You need not agree with the phrasing of the title, and often a good start to an essay analyses the wording of its question. Before you start writing, make rough notes and organise your thoughts so that your finished essay is a tight, relevant and carefully planned piece of writing.

Specimen questions

(1) How does Toni Morrison destroy the reader's sense of security?
(2) *Beloved* 'belongs on the highest shelf of American literature, even if half a dozen canonized white boys have to be elbowed off' (J. Leonard). In what ways is Morrison's novel defined by her status as a black female?
(3) What significance do history and the past have in *Beloved*?
(4) 'I'm interested in survival – who survives, and who does not, and why – and I would like to chart a course that suggests where the dangers are and where the safety might be' (Toni Morrison). Discuss.
(5) What is the role of the character Beloved in the novel of that name?

Specimen answers

(1) How does Toni Morrison destroy the reader's sense of security?

Whether consciously or otherwise, most readers establish a set of rules by which they expect novelists, and thereby literature, to be governed. These rules may never be articulated, but they are endorsed by personal experience and literary convention, a convention that reaches back to Aristotle and has been cherished by many since, that art should be a representation of actuality. In *Beloved* Morrison violates many of these 'rules', though the finished product is indisputably a novel. She dispenses with a linear time-scale and refuses to adhere to temporal or spatial boundaries. The narrative skips backwards or forwards in time, as memories invade and supersede the events of the present. These memories are told in the present tense, such is their vividness. The past is no longer a static and fixed entity, but subject to change and evolution. Morrison's narrative technique is similar to that of Sethe, 'circling the subject' (p. 161). The technique of flashback is common to films. However, while we are accustomed to it on screen, it is much less frequent in literature.

Not only is the reader's sense of time and progression undermined, but Morrison also disregards the concept of restricted consciousness. There is no fixed narrator in *Beloved*. We hear many voices, and Morrison, as an omniscient and omnipresent narrator, enters fully into the consciousness of each of her creations. Furthermore, their memories blend with each other. The second section of the first part of the book begins with Sethe's recollections of her first sexual encounter with her prospective husband, Halle. Her memories are joined by Paul D's thoughts, as he lies beside her in bed. No speech is reported, yet their thoughts coincide and overlap, and, emphasised by the choral repetition of a key-phrase: 'how loose the silk' (p. 27), attain an eerie significance. Paul D remembers watching the corn moving, fully aware of Halle and Sethe's presence and their activity at the bottom of the cornfield. Sethe, back in the present, remembers the corn stalks that broke against Halle's back. There is a description of the men eating the damaged corn that night. The reader realises, at the very end, that we are once again in Paul D's consciousness, signified by the pronoun: 'he'. The next paragraph recounts the reflections of a female character, who, we can only assume, is Sethe, convinced that the preparation of corn is painful. The passage closes with a reference to 'you'. The reader is aware that they are still sharing the thoughts of a character, but it is impossible to be sure to whom these thoughts belong, or to whom they are addressed.

Similarly, Denver begins telling the story of her birth in the third person. Nevertheless the reader hears the story as if Sethe were the narrator. It is difficult to decide whether it is reported conversation or Sethe's experience. The narrative is multiple, and voices shift. The central event of the text, Sethe's murder of her baby daughter to prevent her from living out the horrors imposed by slavery and based on the historical truth of the Margaret Garner story, is treated in an ambivalent manner by Toni Morrison. Sethe's action is described by many characters. We hear Baby Suggs, Schoolteacher, Stamp Paid and Sethe's version of events. No perspective is endorsed by the author, and the reader is left to decide whether or not to approve or comprehend Sethe's action. In the second part of the book there are four sections of stream of consciousness, reporting the internal thoughts of Beloved, Sethe and Denver. The two sections that belong to Beloved are highly confusing. In the first, Morrison shows an utter disregard for typographical conventions. There is no punctuation, while the language is repetitive and the grammar unpredictable. It is difficult to understand the precise points of reference.

These techniques are not new to Morrison. Virginia Woolf manipulates linearity and consciousness in her works, while, a century earlier, Robert Browning (1812–89) played with multi-voiced accounts in *The Ring and the Book* (1868–9). In Morrison's work, however, these techniques have a particularly defamiliarising effect for a reader, augmented by the reader having to accept the existence and power of the supernatural as a given factor in *Beloved*. The text begins with a poltergeist, and the reader, thanks to the pointed clues dotted in the narrative, must come to terms with the fact that one of the characters is a ghost. Moreover, the reader is denied fundamental knowledge. For all the vaunting of the supernatural, we cannot be sure about the exact identity of Beloved. We do not know where she comes from or where she goes. Our ignorance and the limitations of our knowledge are illustrated in our ignorance of the baby girl's name, since Beloved is the name on the gravestone based on the minister's address at the funeral service – 'Dearly Beloved' – and not the baby's given name.

The novel is open-ended, and the reader is even denied a sense of resolution. The story of Beloved is not one to be 'passed on', although that is exactly what Morrison has done. Beloved, by now an embodiment of the horrors of slavery and the haunting effect that the memory of the post-Civil War period has for white and black Americans must not be forgotten. In choosing such a fraught period in which to set her novel, Morrison has gone out of her way to highlight a subject matter that will be disturbing for the reader. The way in which she juxtaposes domestic normality and the repellent memory of injustices, for example, the detailed description of Sethe making biscuits as she describes the sexual and physical abuses to which she was forced to submit, highlights the accepted normality of atrocities for black people of that era. In her interview with Nellie McKay, Morrison states that she desires an emotional response from her readers; that she wants them to be haunted and moved by the stories that she tells. This ambitious intent is fulfilled magnificently in *Beloved*, and the reader, finding their complacent acceptance of literary 'rules' overturned, and their sensibility mauled, can only be disorientated after finishing the last page of *Beloved*.

---

(4) 'I'm interested in survival – who survives, and who does not, and why – and I would like to chart a course that suggests where the dangers are and where the safety might be' (Toni Morrison). Discuss.

Both thematically and linguistically, survival, safety and danger are prominent themes in *Beloved*. Sethe attempts to kill her four children. She defines death as safety, in contradistinction to the danger presented by slavery. Her belief in a life after death allows her to perceive their annihilation in terms of survival. Paul D is struck by her definition of 'safety with a handsaw' and by her confidence that death is preferable to life as a slave. Paul D also acknowledges that it is precisely the sense of safety that is lacking from 124. He believes that this lack was what he felt as he entered the house. As he points out, Sethe's remaining children cannot be said to have been 'saved' by her action: Howard and Buglar leave home and may well be dead, while Denver is too afraid to cross the boundaries of the yard. The realities of white oppression continue and we do not know if Denver will escape their consequences. However Sethe can be counted as one who survives both within the context of the novel and according to Morrison's declaration. She is a literal survivor of Sweet Home and Schoolteacher's methods. She overcomes her past, whilst being a witness to her humiliations destroys her husband. Facing danger, Sethe takes responsibility for her own escape and for her children. She is shunned by her community and yet continues to love and protect her daughter. Her sanity and life are only threatened by the arrival of her dead daughter and by the power of her memories of the past as she is forced to justify her action.

Historically, slavery was a direct attack on black identity and humanity, since it was founded on a denial of both these attributes. Slavery could only exist if slaves were considered to be less than animals, moved around the country with no regard to family ties, and bred for their offspring. Slavery was therefore a test for the survival of a sense of self-worth for black people and can be read as an exploration of the exact location of danger and safety; the charting of the course to which Morrison refers. We see Sethe, trammelled in an exaggerated expression of mother-love, unable to value herself as a 'best thing' so involved is she with the existence of her children. She tells Baby Suggs that she would not draw a breath without them, demonstrating her refusal to value herself outside her role as mother. The novel ends with Sethe's disbelieving cry of 'Me? Me?' and hints at the possibility of a fully realised existence for herself, now that she is purged of her guilt. The woman who perceives ducks to be her children reveals the dangers of succumbing to the bestiality enforced on blacks by whites. Sexual oppression and manipulation, detailed in almost all the accounts of the lives of the women in the novel, presents an extreme danger to self-esteem. It is all too possible to be dirtied and contaminated by prevailing white ideologies. This is what Sethe fears for her daughters.

Stamp Paid challenges white power by renaming himself. This self-baptism is an assertion of self-worth and self-ownership; a direct refutation of slavery. His name alludes to the subtext of commercial exchange that informs the novel; the pricing of Paul D and the other slaves, or Denver's fear that she owes something when she tells the story of her birth. Stamp does not kill his wife, but devotes his life to altruistically helping others. Similarly, Lady Jones, hating herself for her yellow hair, and assuming that this hatred is shared by everyone else, revenges herself on the white people who educate her, by teaching black children how to read and write. Education and knowledge are essential to survival. Halle learns to count in order not to be cheated, and, while Garner lives, succeeds in bartering his commercial worth for the freedom of his mother. Denver's option of attending Oberlin College suggests a survival and safety outside the spectrum of the novel. Lady Jones's self-hatred, exquisitely developed in a paragraph or so, refers to the problems exerted by white identity within the black spectrum. Colourism, or prejudice by the black community against its own members, which is yet another challenge to the survival of black identity, is afforded a more prominent role in Toni Morrison's other novels, in particular, in *Song of Solomon*.

Stamp and Lady Jones, and their chosen methods of survival, emphasise Morrison's vision of 'where the safety might be'. It lies in the black community, in its spiritual and sacred resources. Larger and more encompassing than a restrictive or dysfunctional family unit, the black community is strong and giving. This vision of safety is most fully illustrated by Baby Suggs and her role as 'unchurched preacher'. Baby Suggs and her powerful words in the Clearing, offer an alternative ideology of self-love and self-worth. Under the aegis of her great heart, 124 Bluestone Road is transformed into a focus for love and sharing. It follows therefore, that the greatest danger is a withdrawal from that community, illustrated by Sethe's exclusion, Denver's exile or Baby Suggs's retreat. Nevertheless the community is forgiving, and absorbs even its pariahs. Paul D abandons himself to self-pity, and significantly sitting outside the church, is visited by Stamp who comes to offer him food and lodging. Ella, for all her scorn for Sethe, unites the female community, and saves Sethe, not only from Beloved, but from murdering Mr Bodwin. Denver is reintegrated, and, sheltered to a certain extent from the past of slavery, lends a note of optimism to the novel. We feel that she will survive.

The reader of *Beloved* must confront the unpleasant past of slavery, and acknowledge those who did not survive, whether literally or emotionally. However the novel provides a celebration of the black community's ability, despite the humiliations of its members, to love each other and themselves.

Part 5

Suggestions for further reading

Other novels by Toni Morrison

Jazz, Picador, London, 1993.
Song of Solomon, Picador, London, 1988.
Sula, Picador, London, 1991.
Tar Baby, Picador, London, 1991.
The Bluest Eye, Picador, London, 1990.

Non-fiction works by Toni Morrison

Lecture and Speech of Acceptance, upon the award of the Nobel Prize for Literature, Knopf, Westminster M. D., 1994.
Playing in the Dark: Whiteness and the Literary Imagination, Picador, London, 1993.
'The Site of Memory' in *Inventing the Truth, The Art and Craft of Memoir*, W. Zissner, Houghton Mifflin, Boston, 1987.

Interviews

McKAY, N.: 'An Interview with Toni Morrison', *Contemporary Literature* 24 (Winter 1983) 413–29.
TATE, C.: 'A Conversation with Toni Morrison', *Black Women Writers at Work* Continuum, New York, 1983.
TAYLOR-GUTHRIE, D. (ED.): *Conversations with Toni Morrison*, Roundhouse Publications, Oxford, 1994.

Critical works

BJORK, P.: *The Novels of Toni Morrison: The Search for Self and Place Within the Community*, Lang, 1994.
HEINZE, D.: *The Dilemma of Double Consciousness: Toni Morrison's Novels*, University of Georgia Press, Georgia-Athens, 1993.
RIGNEY, B.: *The Voices of Toni Morrison*, Ohio St. UP, Columbus, 1991.
SAMUELS, W., HUDSON-WEAMS, C.: *Toni Morrison*, G. K. & Hall, Massachusetts, 1990.

Background reading

BOYCE DAVIS, C.: *Black Women, Writing, Identity and the Subject*, Routledge, London, 1994.

CARBY, H.: *Reconstructing Womanhood – The Emergence of the Afro-American Woman Novelist*, Oxford University Press, Oxford, 1995.

CHRISTIAN, B.: *Black Feminist Criticism: Perspectives of Black Women Writers*, Pergamon Press, New York, 1985.

CHRISTIAN, B.: *Black Women Novelists: The Development of a Tradition 1892–1976*, Greenwood Press, Westport, 1980.

DAVIS, C. T., GATES, H. L.: *The Slave's Narrative*, Oxford University Press, Oxford, 1985.

MCDOWELL, D., RAMPERSAD, A.: *Slavery and the Literary Imagination*, John Hopkins, University Press, Baltimore, 1989.

PLASA, C.: *The Discourse of Slavery: Aphra Behn to Toni Morrison*, Routledge, London, 1994.

SMITH, V.: *Self Discovery and Authority in Afro-American Narrative*, Harvard University Press, Cambridge, Mass. 1987.

Other books and articles referred to in the text

ANGELO, B.: 'The Pain of Being Black', *Time*, 22 May 1989.

BLAKE, S.: 'Toni Morrison', from T. Harris, T. Davis (eds) *Afro-American Writers After 1955, The Dictionary of Literary Biography Vol. 33*, Gale Research, Detroit, 1984.

The Guardian, 'The Looting of Language', 9 December 1993.

HEINZE, D.: *The Dilemma of 'Double Consciousness' – Toni Morrison's Novels*, University of Georgia Press, Athens, 1993.

LIDINSKY, A.: 'Prophesying Bodies', from *The Discourse of Slavery* C. Plasa, B. J. Ring (eds), Routledge, London, 1984.

LIDINSKY, A.: *Review of Beloved*, Publisher's Weekly, 17 July 1987.

MORRISON, T. (ED.): MIDDLETON HARRIS, *The Black Book*, Random House, New York, 1974.

RUBIN, M.: Review of *Beloved*, by Toni Morrison, *Christian Science Monitor*, 5 October 1987.

SAUNDERS MOBLEY, M.: 'The Mellow Moods and Difficult Truths of Toni Morrison', *The Southern Review*, Summer 1993.

The author of these notes

Laura Gray is the author of York Notes on *Roll of Thunder, Hear My Cry* by Mildred D. Taylor. She was born in Scotland and studied English at Somerville College, Oxford. She is currently working in Italy.